SAVE $ ON YOUR HOME MORTGAGE

SAVE $ ON YOUR HOME MORTGAGE:
Mortgage Acceleration Techniques

MICHAEL C. THOMSETT

WILEY

JOHN WILEY & SONS

New York • Chichester • Brisbane • Toronto • Singapore

This publication is designed to provide accurate and authoritative information in regard to the subject matter covered. It is sold with the understanding that the publisher is not engaged in rendering legal, accounting, or other professional service. If legal advice or other expert assistance is required, the services of a competent professional person should be sought. *From a Declaration of Principles jointly adopted by a Committee of the American Bar Association and a Committee of Publishers.*

Library of Congress Cataloging-in-Publication Data:

Thomsett, Michael C.

Save $ on your home mortgage: Mortgage acceleration techniques / by Michael C. Thomsett.

p. cm.

Includes index.

ISBN 0-471-50062-3.—ISBN 0-471-50063-1 (pbk.)

1. Mortgage loans. 2. Prepayment of debts. I. Title.

II. Title: Save dollars on your home mortgage: Mortgage acceleration techniques

HG2040.15.T48 1989

332.7′2—dc19 88-27607

CIP

Printed in the United States of America

10 9 8 7 6 5 4 3 2 1

CONTENTS

INTRODUCTION: THE REAL COST OF HOUSING

"Buying your own home is the best investment you can make." Everyone who has thought about buying real estate has heard this statement. But in fact, the observation must be qualified: Once you have made your purchase, the method you use to pay off your mortgage determines how good an investment you have actually made.

Equity—the value of your home that is free of debt—is built up in four ways: first, from the down payment you make when you buy; second, from principal payments to the lender; third, from permanent improvements you make to your property; and fourth, from increases in market value.

The subject of this book is increasing and managing the equity that you build by decreasing your mortgage. Even with the strong historical performance of residential real estate, a harsh reality is that in many instances it is the lender rather than the homeowner who profits from increased market value in real estate. In the typical 30-year fixed-rate mortgage plan, your total payments can be as high as two and one-half to three times the purchase price. So even if your $100,000 house increases in value to $250,000 over the years, the investment benefit will have gone to the lender (in the form of interest) rather than to you, the buyer.

This problem arises from the fact that interest represents the greater part of mortgage payments during the early years of the mortgage. It takes many years to accumulate any real equity in your home under the long-term repayment plan.

The solution is to devise a method for accelerating the rate of repayment. This book shows you how to achieve significant savings over time by devising a systematic, affordable method for managing your mortgage.

Your home is primarily a personal asset rather than an investment. Even so, there is an investment question to be answered. If you are paying on a mortgage and also making other investments, you should compare the rate of return and risks. The yield from other investments might not be as high as the yield produced by accelerating repayment of your home mortgage.

There are arguments against acceleration. It reduces your tax deduction for interest. It ties up money that would otherwise be available in the event of a personal emergency. And in some situations, you can earn a higher rate of return by putting your money in other investments.

These issues are addressed in this book. The first three chapters explain how mortgages work and how the relationship between interest and equity affects the total real cost of buying your home. Chapters 4 through 6 explain how various acceleration plans are devised and what outcome you will achieve with them.

Chapter 7 explains the need for creating an emergency reserve fund as a priority, before putting additional money into principal payments. Chapter 8 explains how the common arguments against acceleration often are flawed. And the last four chapters offer suggestions for selecting mortgages, refinancing, and staying in control as you build home equity over the years.

Appendix 1 lists amortization tables from 8 to 15 percent, showing the monthly payment that must be made on mortgages. Appendix 2 summarizes the remaining balances—that portion of debt still outstanding at the end of each year in the mortgage term. And Appendix 3 shows how several typical plans reduce interest costs and repayment time. Finally, the glossary lists important loan and mortgage terms.

The purpose of this book is not to claim that every homeowner will benefit from embarking upon a plan for paying off a mortgage. This book presents a series of mathematical facts about the true cost of housing, compares acceleration and outside investments, and demonstrates how substantial savings can be achieved over time. You will see why many of the common arguments against acceleration and building equity may be contrary to your goal of accumulating equity and reducing taxes. Some of the arguments are

1. If you pay off your mortgage more rapidly than required, you will reduce the tax advantage of paying interest.

2. Rather than accelerating, you should use your money for investments that yield a higher rate of return.

3. It's foolish to let your equity sit in your home. That idle money should be put to work.

Lenders (who profit from interest) and financial advisors (who depend on commission income) often advise homeowners to refinance or to pay off a mortgage over the longest possible term, suggestions that benefit someone other than yourself. These arguments are convincing, but the whole story is not always told. This book will show how the relationship between equity and cost actually works, leaving it to you to make an *informed* decision. Armed with information, you can proceed with knowledge and confidence toward achieving your financial goals and profiting from owning your home.

SAVE $ ON YOUR HOME MORTGAGE

1 FACTS ABOUT MORTGAGES

A family shopping for a home usually concentrates on the purchase price. Affordability is thought of in terms of list prices and what the list price means in terms of a down payment and continuing monthly payments on a mortgage.

A reality of buying a home is that the contracted price represents only a small portion of that home's total cost. Affordability is not limited to the immediate question of list price but also includes the longer-term total cost of purchase. When you finance your home with a mortgage, you will pay two to three times more than the agreed price, in the form of interest.

As discouraging as that might seem, there is another fact that many homeowners overlook: The ultimate cost of your home can be determined, planned, and controlled by you, the owner. Once you realize the cost of financing a purchase over many years, a natural reaction might be to shrug and ask What can I do?

With a carefully planned program of mortgage acceleration, you can do quite a lot. You can reduce your interest costs and determine not only the total price but the future date on which you will own your home free and clear.

INTEREST ON YOUR MORTGAGE

The interest on the traditional mortgage well exceeds the actual purchase price. Using a rate of 10 percent as an example, a 30-year mortgage actually costs you 316 percent more than the amount you borrowed. So if your financed balance is $80,000, your total payments add up to $252,742.

Why is the total cost so high? Interest is figured each month based on the amount of debt outstanding. So at the beginning of the term, the entire amount is subject to interest. In the earlier years of repayment, the debt moves downward very slowly.

Accelerating your mortgage—paying additional money against the loan amount—reduces interest over time. This process can produce some big savings. For example,

1. You will reduce the cost of your home by as much as $100,000 by paying your mortgage over 15 years rather than 30 years—and more if the interest rate is high.

2. Your 30-year loan is only one-half paid off by the 24th year. Most of the payments you make until that point go to interest.

3. Every reduction in interest costs translates to greater profits for you. The amount you earn when you sell your house depends not only on current market value but also on the amount of equity you have built up. And acceleration builds equity.

4. Making a 13th payment at the beginning of your 30-year mortgage term reduces the repayment period by one full year.

5. Paying an extra $25 per month on an $80,000 mortgage (at 10 percent on a 30-year term) will take five years off the repayment period and reduce your cost by more than $34,000.

6. Paying an extra $100 per month on the same mortgage will take 12 years off the repayment period and reduce your cost by more than $80,000.

The degree to which you reduce the cost of buying your house depends on the type of acceleration plan you adopt. Keep in mind that you have the opportunity to decide how much to pay for your house. With a carefully devised plan for acceleration, you have the power of controlling your financial future, including both total cost and timing of repayment.

THE ATTRIBUTES OF THE MORTGAGE

The higher the interest rate, the longer the term, and the more you borrow, the greater the amount of total interest you will pay. A mortgage has three main attributes, each one affecting your home's cost.

The Amount Borrowed

The loan amount itself will determine how much interest you pay. Interest on a $50,000 loan will be much lower than that on a $100,000 loan.

In evaluating your total cost of housing, the amount borrowed is your first consideration, for a number of reasons. First, the lender will grant the loan only if you qualify (your income must be high enough so that you can afford the payments). To qualify for their first mortgages, many people agree to long-term financing on their homes. The traditional 30-year fixed-rate mortgage is the favorite way to finance a home, even with the widespread proliferation of variable-rate loans.

The Payment Term

The second attribute is the amount of time it will take to repay your mortgage. The longer the term, the lower the monthly payment—but the greater the interest cost.

A 30-year fixed-rate mortgage is widely thought to be advantageous to you, the borrower and buyer. That's because your housing costs will be fixed over the next three decades. During those years, it's reasonable to expect some degree of inflation. It's also reasonable to expect your income to rise. With those two facts in mind, a permanent, fixed cost of housing actually reduces your costs over time.

Example. You and your spouse purchase a home and sign an agreement for an $80,000 mortgage, to be repaid over 30 years at the rate of 10 percent. Your monthly payments will be $702.06. Your total monthly family income is $2,900 per month. But you and your spouse expect to earn more money as you advance in your careers. If, in 10 years, your family income increases to $4,500 per month, you have an advantage in your fixed-rate mortgage. At the time you signed the contract, the payments represented 24 percent of your monthly pay. Now, that same payment is less than 16 percent.

The Interest Rate

The total cost of interest is also affected by the interest rate on your loan. The difference made by a seemingly small change in the effective rate can be substantial.

Example. A 2 percent difference in interest rates can be costly. If you borrow $80,000 at 10 percent, total interest over 30 years is $172,742. But if you pay 12 percent, interest is $43,500 more.

From 1978 through 1988, mortgage interest rates varied from 7 to 20 percent. This wide swing was caused by several economic conditions, including the rate banks could earn by investing cash in different places, the federal discount and prime rates, and the level of controls the Federal Reserve placed on the money supply. Figure 1–1 compares interest costs at various rates of interest.

The amount, term, and rate combine to determine what you will actually pay for your home. Mortgage acceleration reduces your cost by eliminating part of the term, the most significant factor in the total equation. With a shorter-term mortgage, the amount of debt is reduced more rapidly; as a result, the total interest is reduced, often by $100,000 or more.

Compare the total cost of interest, again using the example of

	INTEREST RATE			
30–YEAR TERM:	8%	10%	12%	14%
amount borrowed	$ 80,000	$ 80,000	$ 80,000	$ 80,000
interest	131,327	172,742	216,244	261,244
total paid	211,327	252,742	296,244	341,244

Figure 1–1 Total mortgage costs

10 percent on an $80,000 debt. Interest over 30 years is $172,742. Under the terms of a 15-year mortgage, the same loan includes $74,744, or a savings of $97,998.

THE FLEXIBILITY OF YOUR PLAN

A realistic mortgage acceleration plan must remain flexible. The limitations of a personal budget make this flexibility a necessity.

For the home buyer who has a limited amount of cash each month, acceleration might seem impractical. Many first-time buyers, for example, can barely afford to cover their expenses each month. All their cash went into the down payment and closing costs, the monthly payment itself is higher than rent they previously paid, and both spouses must work just to meet the family's obligations.

These problems require realistic solutions. No theory can work unless it's affordable, so suggesting that you double your payment or even that you add $100 per month makes no sense unless it works within the limitations of your budget.

One of the attractive features of mortgage acceleration is that it's a voluntary plan. You're in control. You decide if and when to make additional payments, and you can start and stop the plan at any time you want. If you commit yourself to a short-term mortgage by contract, you must then make your monthly payment every month. But when you are obligated to a 30-year repayment schedule, you have the *choice* of paying off that loan more rapidly.

For many families, acceleration comes about when monthly income rises to the point that it's affordable. Remembering that a fixed-rate mortgage freezes your monthly payments at the contracted level, growth in your income means greater flexibility. Family finances typically follow a predictable pattern:

1. When you are young and just beginning a career, your income is minimal, and you have no cash, savings, or investments. You can barely meet expenses each month.
2. Several years later, your income has risen enough so that

you can save money for a down payment. Your first house places a drain on your finances and might also deplete both your savings and all the flexibility in your budget.

3. Once your housing costs are frozen, future increases in income introduce flexibility back into your budget. At this point, you have enough income to put some money into savings and investments.

At the point that you can afford to begin saving money, an acceleration plan will become most practical.

In a sense, reducing the interest costs of buying your home is an investment. Every dollar you put into reducing your mortgage balance "earns" the rate of interest in effect, because you are reducing your future interest expense by that same rate.

Example. Your interest rate is 10 percent. You pay $100 each month above the required payment to be applied against the loan balance. Because these payments will reduce future interest by 10 percent of the outstanding balance, the effect is the same as that of earning 10 percent on another investment.

With this in mind, acceleration—as an investment—should be compared to what you can earn by saving or investing elsewhere. But a second feature must be included in the comparison. You might be able to earn 12 percent by putting that $100 per month into an investment. But how much risk will you take? All investments include some degree of risk, but when you accelerate your mortgage, risk is minimal. Because you live in your house, insure it, and maintain its condition, you tend the investment every day. A comparably low risk will be difficult, if not impossible, to find elsewhere. Investments and risks are compared in more detail in Chapter 8.

THE SLOW RATE OF REPAYMENT

To fully realize the extent of the cost of a 30-year mortgage, you should know how your balance falls over time. Most first-time home buyers keep their homes for five years or less. Under the traditional mortgage plan, they pay less than 4 percent of their loan during those early years.

During periods when real estate values rise very rapidly, it is possible to earn a profit from keeping a house for only a few years. But you must remember that demand is cyclical and cannot be depended on when you buy your home. A second point is that your home is primarily a personal asset and not an investment. The consideration of profit should not be a motivating factor in the timing and selection of a home purchase. But because the cost of that personal asset can be controlled, and is significant, you should be concerned with the long-term total cost and the methods you can employ to control it.

As a homeowner, the question of total cost is an important one. That question extends to the amount of equity you will accumulate over time and how the timing of eliminating a mortgage will affect your financial future.

Example. A couple purchases a home and commits to a 30-year mortgage. However, both plan to retire in 20 years. They must either budget for retirement with a continuing obligation to make mortgage payments or plan ahead and reduce the repayment term.

With a 30-year mortgage (assuming 10 percent), the percentage due on your mortgage at the end of each year demonstrates the extent of the problem in slowly declining balances. See Figure 1–2.

At the end of the fifth year (the point where most first-time owners sell), 96.6 percent of the original loan is still due. And after 10 years, 90.9 percent remains outstanding. In fact, one-half of the total debt is not even paid off by the 24th year.

What does this mean in terms of dollars spent versus the accumulation of equity? By the end of the fifth year on an $80,000 loan, the total amount paid adds up to $42,124, more than half of the original amount loaned. But only $2,741 has gone to principal. The remainder, $39,380, is interest.

After 10 years, you will have paid $84,247 to the lender, or more than the original amount of the loan. But at that point, only $7,250 has gone to principal reduction and $76,999 has gone to

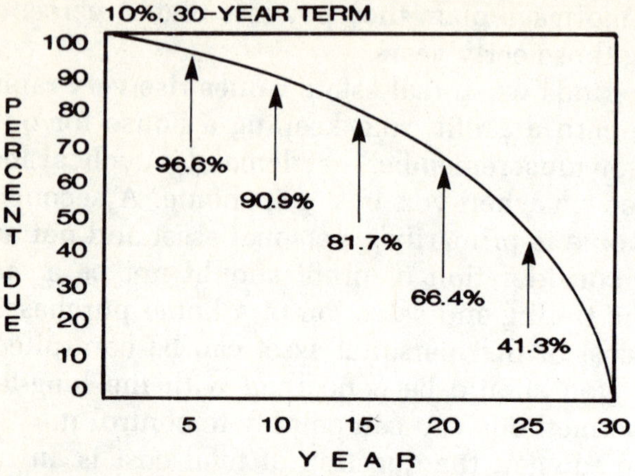

Figure 1–2 Outstanding mortgage percentages

interest. Total payments and principal reduction are compared in Figure 1–3.

To figure out the amount of outstanding debt on your mortgage, look at the percentages on a remaining balance table. Appendix 2 includes interest tables from 8 to 15 percent.

Refer to the table for the interest rate you pay on your mortgage. (If your rate falls between the quarter-percentage rate tables shown, estimate your remaining balance as an average of the tables above and below your rate.)

The 10 percent table, for example, shows the following information:

1. The age of the loan is listed in the first column. Calculate the number of years since you bought your house, and find the appropriate line.

2. Across the top, the original term is listed. This is the number of years you have to pay off your mortgage. For example, the column labeled "30" is for 30-year loans.

3. The percentage shown in the "30" column, on the line corresponding to the age of your loan, is the degree remaining on your loan. For example, after the fifth year, the percentage

$80,000 LOAN, 10%, 30-YEAR TERM

year	payments to date	interest to date	principal to date
1	$ 8,425	$ 7,977	$ 445
2	16,849	15,913	936
3	25,274	23,794	1,479
4	33,699	31,619	2,078
5	42,124	39,380	2,741
10	84,247	76,999	7,250
15	126,371	111,699	14,670
20	168,494	141,622	26,877
25	210,618	163,658	46,962
30	252,742	172,742	80,000

Figure 1–3 Interest and principal

shown is 96.6. Therefore, on an $80,000 original loan, you owe approximately $77,280 after five years:

$$\$80{,}000 \times 96.6\% = \$77{,}280$$

ADVANTAGES OF ACCELERATION

Any extra payments you make to reduce your mortgage balance are immediately "tied up" in the form of home equity. Unlike a savings account, you cannot later decide you need that money and take it back.

This factor can work either as a benefit or a handicap, depending on how well you plan your program. It is essential that you determine—before making any payments—that you can afford the plan and will not need that money in the near future. If you do have to take it back out, the only way is to refinance or commit to a second mortgage. Either way, it's expensive to reverse the plan.

As an advantage, acceleration is a form of forced savings. You will not be tempted to use the money invested in home equity, because you cannot put your hands on it easily or quickly. In comparison, money in a savings account at your local bank can be taken out quite easily—a reality known to most of us already.

As a disadvantage, committing part of your monthly budget to such a permanent form of savings can have severe economic consequences for you and your family. Because of these consequences, a responsible mortgage acceleration plan should be started only after you have also established an emergency reserve fund. You should have some cash saved up and easily available in a bank account, money market fund, or some other very liquid (available) investment. Some advisors suggest three months' income as a minimum; others say six. The level that's right for you depends on your total family income, whether or not your spouse also works, and the types of expenses you have. If you are committed to many debts on credit cards, auto loans, and personal loans besides your mortgage, your monthly financial burden is greater than if you have no other debts. And your emergency reserve fund will have to be greater to accommodate your commitments.

Some advisors argue that you should not accelerate your mortgage but should pay it over the longest possible term and invest available cash elsewhere. This argument might apply in some situations, but only if you are willing to trade the relatively low risk of acceleration for greater risks of other investments—and only if you have the discipline to leave your money in another investment.

If the mathematical facts concerning mortgage interest over a long term are examined, the argument against acceleration does not always make sense. However, a true comparison is not always made for a number of reasons.

1. The comparison is not entirely tangible. The factor of risk cannot be put down on paper, and even an investment that looks safe might represent a much higher risk than acceleration.

2. The security factor is not built into the comparison. By accelerating your mortgage, you increase equity more rapidly,

meaning that you own a greater portion of your house in a shorter period of time. That gives you and your family personal security, a point that advisors often miss when suggesting that acceleration is unwise.

3. When you build equity, you profit from reduced interest over your repayment term. But that does not generate a commission for your advisor. And advisors are compensated by a commission, based on the amount of money you invest—a reality that naturally adds a conflict of interest to any advice you get from a salesperson.

ACCELERATION IN THE TOTAL PLAN

There are valid arguments against acceleration in certain economic conditions. For example, when you have a very low fixed rate but you can earn substantially more by investing elsewhere—given that the differences in risk are acceptable to you—it is prudent to stretch your mortgage payments over the full term. And if you cannot afford to tie up your money in any investment as permanent as your home equity, acceleration won't make sense for you.

The arguments against an accelerated plan must certainly be addressed and are dealt with in other chapters. But you will benefit from acceleration if you meet these criteria:

You can afford to place some money in long-term investments.

You have established an emergency reserve fund.

You are not willing to accept higher risks for comparable rates of return.

You want to pay off your mortgage well before the contracted due date.

Most homeowners in fact, will discover that some level of acceleration is wise. It will yield a higher rate of return than other investments for much less risk and will actually eliminate the risk of owing money.

The risk you live with by carrying a mortgage is worth adding to the equation. In comparing one investment against another, remember that risk comes in many forms. Owing money to a lender for the next 30 years is a significant form of risk. In the event that you are disabled and cannot work, will your family be able to keep the house? If you lose your job, have unexpected medical costs, or change careers, what will happen to your family budget?

The earlier you are able to eliminate a mortgage debt, the less risk you carry. In the meantime, there are several steps you can take to deal with that risk. You can carry adequate life, health, and disability insurance, so that unexpected loss of income will not threaten your family's security. And you can set up an emergency reserve fund and invest in a diversified portfolio of securities.

The combination of insurance (for protection) and savings or investments (for financial security) is a natural and prudent strategy in a personal financial plan. But buying your home, which is the largest single expenditure most families undertake, is a major factor in your personal finances—and the cost of interest plays an important role in determining your ultimate net worth and financial security. The idea of mortgage acceleration, combined with the other financial decisions you make, should not be overlooked as a valid strategy.

Among the arguments against acceleration is the claim that it reduces tax benefits. We will deal with this question in greater detail in Chapter 8. For now, the point to be made is that any valid comparison should be made on an after-tax basis. But remember that investing money somewhere else will produce taxable income. Thus, whether you *earn* money from wise investments or *reduce* costs through acceleration, there is a tax consequence.

The tax argument is flawed because it overlooks one inescapable reality: that tax deductions are *not* more advantageous than reduced costs. For example, if your effective tax rate is 28 percent, your taxes will be reduced by 28 percent of the deductible interest you pay each year. So if your total interest expense next year is $6,000, you gain a tax deduction of $1,680. The net cost after taxes is

$6,000 − $1,680 = $4,320

If, through acceleration, you reduce next year's interest cost to $4,000, the net cost is

$4,000 − $1,120 = $2,880

The anti-acceleration argument is that you lose from lower interest write-offs. In the example above, acceleration reduces the tax benefit by $560. But of greater significance is the fact that the net after-tax cost of interest has been reduced by $1,440 ($4,320 versus $2,880).

No financial decision should be based on the argument that you need tax deductions. As long as your tax rate is lower than 100 percent, the benefits of reduced costs always exceed the benefit of higher deductions. No matter what rate you use to test this fact, the result is always the same: *Lower costs, even tax-deductible costs, are more advantageous than the deductions themselves.*

WHY LENDERS LIKE ACCELERATION

Advisors, compensated by commissions, do not like the idea of mortgage acceleration. It does not produce any income for them. Many arguments used by salespeople are aimed at convincing you to use leverage (borrowed money) to achieve some type of result. Unlike advisors, though, lenders benefit from acceleration because it reduces their risks.

From the lender's point of view, any time a mortgage is granted, there is a risk. You might not make your monthly payments, forcing the lender to foreclose on your property to get its money back.

Foreclosure is not a desirable outcome. For the lender, it means devoting time and energy to finding a buyer. And chances are, the lender will not be able to recover its investment. As a general rule, homes that are foreclosed often are poorly maintained, even abused. To get a home into marketable condition, the lender might have to hire contractors to repair the property. That means investing more money.

Another reality is that foreclosures are higher in areas where property values are not rising, where owners do not care for their properties, and where crime rates are high. All these facts make it difficult to sell properties. The lender might be unable to sell at a profit or, even worse, might not be able to find a buyer at all.

Lenders require a down payment so that homeowners have a stake in their properties. If you did not put money into the home purchase, it would be fairly easy to walk away from it whenever you wanted. But with money on the line, you have equity. And the higher your equity, the lower the risks for the lender. The total outstanding loan balance represents an increasingly greater portion of the home's current market value, so that the risk of foreclosure is lower.

In the event of foreclosure on a home in which equity is high, the lender will also have a better than average chance of recovering its own investment. So from the lender's point of view, acceleration makes the outstanding loan a better risk.

You will not have difficulty making additional payments with most lenders. Many lenders even include a line on your monthly payment bill for extra payments, as in this sample:

Payment due:	
Principal	$ 47.72
Interest	654.34
Total due	$702.06
Additional payment:	
Impounds	______
Principal	______
Amount enclosed	$______

Even though lenders benefit from acceleration, most mortgage loans contain a provision for a prepayment penalty. If you pay your mortgage too rapidly, you are penalized. This provision is contradictory to the idea of reducing risk through greater equity buildup and is based on the idea that a lender earning a profit on interest does not want to lose that interest due to early payment.

The prepayment penalty will be waived in some situations. For example, a lender granted a 30-year fixed-rate mortgage in 1972 at the rate of 7.5 percent. Several years later, when the going rate was much higher, the lender viewed that low-rate mortgage in a different light. So the lender offered to refinance the mortgage at a higher rate, with incentives like preapproval for a higher amount of money, no appraisal fee, and, of course, no prepayment penalty on the older note.

The prepayment penalty was devised in the days when interest rates were fairly consistent and dependable and fixed-rate loans were the norm. Today, though, with widespread use of variable-rate loans, widely varying rates on the market, and much less certainty about future rates, the prepayment penalty is antiquated but still in use.

Typically, the terms of a mortgage will allow you to pay off no more than 20 or 25 percent of your total mortgage balance in any one year. So at a maximum, you could pay off your entire mortgage in four or five years, if you had the cash available. Under most of the conditions of gradual acceleration, the prepayment penalty will not be a problem, nor should it affect the economic benefits of the plan.

When you negotiate your mortgage with the lender, you will be able to contract for a lower rate if you offer to pay over a shorter term. For example, one savings and loan association advertises fixed-rate mortgages for 10.25 percent over 30 years or for 9.75 percent over 15 years.

The lower rate offered for shorter-term loans reflects the lender's awareness of risk. A longer term means greater risks, in two respects. First, the sooner the mortgage is paid off (and the more rapidly equity builds up), the less the likelihood of loan default. Second, the shorter the term of a fixed-rate loan, the lower the chance that the effective interest rate will fall below the market rate.

Consider the problems for lenders who wrote a large volume of loans before 1975. Rates varied between 5 and 7 percent. However, by 1980, mortgages were going for as high as 20 percent. In that inflated economy, the outstanding balances that yielded the lower rates created losses. If the lender's cost of acquiring money is greater than the yield on an outstanding loan, the lender has a loss rather than a profit. For this reason, lenders today prefer shorter-term mortgages and will provide incentives through lower rates.

The key to understanding the true cost of buying your home is in knowing how interest and equity work. You don't pay just the purchase price; the real cost of your home is actually determined by the amount of interest you pay. And that's something that is within your control. The next chapter deals with the relationship between equity and interest—and the advantage that gives you as a homeowner.

2 INTEREST AND EQUITY: WHO REALLY PROFITS?

You can determine the total cost of your home, as we saw in the last chapter. One myth about buying a house is that the price the seller and buyer agree to is, in fact, the "cost" of a home. In fact, the amount of interest you pay over the years is a more significant factor in arriving at total cost.

A second myth is that homeowners build equity mainly from increases in market value. While market value may increase significantly over the years you own your home, much of it is converted to profits for the lender. True, home values increase as the result of demand, but you cannot depend on that growth.

A third myth is that you're better off paying full interest on your mortgage, to get the maximum value of itemized deductions on your tax return. In fact, lower cost is always worth more than higher deductions, on an after-tax basis.

You will build more equity by reducing the interest cost of buying a home. As long as market value exceeds the interest you pay to the lender, your equity continues to rise. But the lender will still make a greater profit on your home than you will, as long as you're paying a mortgage over the long term.

SOURCES OF EQUITY

You can adopt one of two attitudes concerning the buildup of equity in your home. The first and most common attitude is that equity results from increased market value, combined with the gradual repayment of a mortgage loan. The second attitude is that you can directly control the cost of buying your home and create equity for yourself.

The passive attitude, as we will demonstrate later in this chapter, is a costly one. It results in the lender earning a greater profit on your home than you do.

Equity does, indeed, increase as the result of greater demand for homes like yours. If you buy a home for $100,000 and, 10 years later, sell at a profit, you have gained from the demand factor. In the past, housing in many areas was invariably a sound and profitable investment, because housing prices climbed every year.

Besides the actual demand for homes—the number of potential buyers versus available homes—other factors contribute to market value. They include the location of your home, the cost to build new homes, and the degree of care and maintenance you and your neighbors put into your properties.

In neighborhoods where owners occupy their own homes, perform ongoing maintenance, and take pride in their property, market values sustain and build. But in areas where most homes are rented out, maintenance is not performed, and crime rates are high, values will not rise as quickly—they could even fall.

If employment rates decline in your area, many people will want to sell their homes and move away. That will create a market where the supply is greater than the demand, and housing prices must fall as a result. This situation has occurred many times in the past, notably in regions where one industry accounted for a high degree of employment and large-scale layoffs occurred. For example, Texas and Louisiana homeowners suffered when oil and oil service industry employment fell. The Detroit area's economy is sensitive to trends in auto manufacturing. And the Pacific Northwest is very dependent on defense contracting employers. All these regions have suffered economic problems in the past, including falling housing prices.

Housing values, to a large extent, are dependent on the prevailing economic circumstances. When employment demand is up, people move to the area and buy homes. And when employment falls, families are forced to sell and move elsewhere. The assumption that your house's value and equity will rise automatically is not always a completely safe one.

Another source of equity is home improvement. You can add a new room to your home, for example, by borrowing money secured by equity. That addition adds to market value, to an extent. Improvements undertaken to expand living space or to improve your family's comfort are sound investments. But if you improve only to increase equity, you could run into a problem.

There is a limit on the benefits of improving your home. If you purchase a property with three bedrooms and two baths, for example, the ultimate sale price you can expect will be limited to the prices of comparable homes in the same area—even if you have improved your home well beyond the original floor plan.

Example. In your area, homes like yours have sold recently for $90,000 to $110,000. You have spent $30,000 on improvements during the last five years. You cannot expect to sell your home for $130,000 or $140,000 just because you have added value to it. You might get more than the average price for comparable homes. But if you over-improve, the maximum sale price will be limited. Buyers will not be willing to pay a price very far above that of comparable homes, and you probably will not be able to sell for an amount equal to the total cost of improvements.

The amount of equity you will build in your home, as a result of market conditions and improvements, is both limited and uncertain. You are at the mercy of economic conditions and have little control over demand.

Assuming, though, that you do depend on continuing demand for houses like yours, the question remains, Who will profit from an increase in equity? To find the answer to this question, you should compare the historical changes in housing prices to the cost of buying and borrowing.

COMPARING PROFITS

Equity builds gradually through reducing your debt. But that form of equity accumulates very slowly in the early years of a 30-year repayment term, and the likelihood of a substantial profit is lower when you sell after only 5 or 10 years.

Example. Two individuals buy homes at about the same time, each paying $100,000. They both make a down payment of $20,000, or 20 percent of the purchase price. Ten years later, both sell. The first owner gets $140,000, and the second sells for $120,000.

To compare the actual net profit on each of these transactions, we'll assume that the buyers' closing costs equal 3 percent of the purchase price and that the sellers' commission and closing costs equal 8 percent. We'll also assume that both had the same mortgage terms—10 percent on a 30-year term.

The first homeowner will realize a net profit of $25,800 on the sale—the adjusted sale proceeds of $128,800, minus an adjusted basis of $103,000. The second homeowner will realize only $7,400.

A second way to compare these two cases is on the basis of the amount of cash each seller gets. This calculation is done by reducing the net proceeds by the outstanding mortgage balance and then subtracting the original down payment. This *cash profit* is a fair comparison as long as both individuals paid the same amount on their mortgages. The outcome of each case is summarized in Figure 2–1.

In this comparison, we have not considered the interest cost on paying on a mortgage for 10 years. The comparison is valid, however, as long as both homeowners paid the same amount. The total of 10 years' payments would be $84,247, based on a payment schedule of $702.06 per month.

With this exercise, you can see the problem of paying on a mortgage in the hopes of realizing a profit upon sale. The first homeowner's property increased in value by 40 percent over the 10 years. Yet, even though $84,247 in payments were made, the

	homeowner 1	homeowner 2
PROFIT		
sale price	$140,000	$120,000
less: closing costs	11,200	9,600
net proceeds	$128,800	$110,400
purchase price	$100,000	$100,000
plus: closing costs	3,000	3,000
total cost	$103,000	$103,000
profit on sale →	$ 25,800	$ 7,400
CASH		
net proceeds	$128,800	$110,400
mortgage balance	72,750	72,750
cash to seller	$ 56,050	$ 37,650
less: down payment	20,000	20,000
cash profit →	$ 36,050	$ 17,650

Figure 2–1 Profit in 10 years

adjusted profit on the sale was only $25,800. Although those payments represented 84 percent of the original purchase price, the owner accumulated only $7,250 in equity.

The lender, in comparison, made a profit of $76,996 in interest. That's about three times more profit for the lender than for the homeowner.

In the case of the second homeowner, the gap is even wider. The homeowner made a profit of $7,400, or about one-tenth of the amount the lender earned.

HOMEOWNER AND LENDER PROFITS

If you pay a long-term mortgage without any form of equity control, then the lender does, in fact, make a greater profit than you will. This reality is one that you can either accept or change.

Rather than allowing the majority of your equity to convert to lender profits, you can increase your own equity by controlling the ultimate price of your home. You should consider planning and controlling your interest cost in the same way that you would evaluate an investment.

Your home, as a personal asset, should not be evaluated just on an investment basis. You must consider your career, schools and friends your children make, the trauma of uprooting a family too often, and the costs of buying and selling—all the considerations that determine where you live and how long you stay. In other words, quality of life is more important for you as a homeowner than the quality (profit potential) of an investment.

The comparison, however, is one that should be made when determining whether to proceed with a plan of mortgage acceleration, whether you plan to move in the near future or stay where you are for the rest of your life. If you have money available to invest, you should compare outside investments (mutual funds, stocks, other real estate) and reduction of interest costs on your home.

Referring back to the previous example of the two homeowners, compare one more factor: how much they profited versus how much the lender profited.

The first homeowner realized a profit of $25,800, or 25 percent of the original adjusted cost, averaging out to 2.5 percent per year, and the second homeowner earned 7.2 percent, or less than 1 percent per year. But the lender, who loaned $80,000, made a profit of 96.2 percent—a yearly average of 9.6 percent (Fig. 2–2).

Just as the homeowners received proceeds upon sale, the lender received proceeds represented by the total of payments made. The substantial differences in investment value between the buyers and the lender make the point: Under traditional long-term

	homeowner 1	homeowner 2	lender
net proceeds	$128,800	$110,400	$156,997
basis	103,000	103,000	80,000
profit on sale	$ 25,800	$ 7,400	$ 76,997
% profit	25.0%	7.2%	96.2%
yearly average	2.5%	0.7%	9.6%

Figure 2–2 Comparing profits

mortgage arrangements, real estate is more profitable for the lender than for the homeowner.

A lender is unlikely to draw this disparity in profits to your attention. It shows, however, that real estate—as profitable an investment as it may be—is not as profitable as lending money. If confronted with the facts, lenders will defend themselves by claiming that they take a greater risk than buyers because, if loans are defaulted, they stand to lose money. But because mortgage loans are secured by real estate, the truth is that lenders take very minimal risks. The homeowner invests in the form of a down payment and contributes to equity over time. Both buyer and lender share risk in its various forms, but the lender makes a greater profit.

You do not have to simply accept this situation as a fact of life. By controlling the amount of interest you pay, you will build equity more quickly and earn value by reducing the actual cost of buying your home. One form of accelerating your mortgage is by contracting to pay it over 15 years rather than 30 years. On an $80,000 mortgage, monthly payments at 10 percent are

Term	Payments
15 years	$859.69
30 years	702.06
Difference	$157.63

Over the entire term of each mortgage, the totals of all payments are

Term	Payments
15 years	$154,744
30 years	252,742
Difference	97,998

In this form of mortgage acceleration, a homeowner will increase equity by nearly $98,000 and pay off the entire debt in half the time—all for an additional payment of $157.63 per month.

THE INFLATION FACTOR

To this point, we have discussed three popular myths about buying a home. First is the idea that the agreed-upon price of a home is what it actually costs; second, that equity builds mainly from increases in market value; and third, that you benefit from deducting full interest on your tax return.

A fourth myth is that having a fixed-rate mortgage protects you from inflation, so it is not necessary to be concerned about the cost of interest.

The fact is, inflation makes buying a home a good investment in comparison to paying rent, but it does not make mortgage acceleration a bad idea.

A renter's cost of housing goes up over the years, as the landlord raises rent to reflect increasing market value and as demand for apartments grows. If you assume that inflation grows at the rate of 2 percent per year, it's also reasonable to assume that, on average, rental costs will also increase by 2 percent per year.

A buyer who finances a home with a fixed-rate mortgage benefits from inflation in the same way. The cost of housing decreases over time. Again by using 2 percent inflation as an example, it's reasonable to assume that average income (if it keeps pace) will grow by 2 percent of the inflation rate. At the same time, that buyer's housing costs are fixed.

So inflation must be evaluated in two ways. First, the buying power of the dollar is eroded as prices climb. At 2 percent inflation, $1 today will buy only $0.82 cents worth of goods in 10 years. Second, the cost of goods rises due to inflation. At 2 percent, something that costs $1 today will cost $1.22 in 10 years.

Applied to the renting versus buying argument, both methods of judging the cost of inflation must be used. The renter must pay ever-increasing amounts for housing (increased cost), while the homeowner's cost is reduced through fixed payments (buying power).

Example. A renter pays $600 per month for an apartment. Average rent increases match inflation at the rate of 2 percent per year. Ten years later, the same apartment costs $732 per month.

Example. A buyer must make mortgage payments of $702 per month. These payments represent 23.4 percent of the family's monthly income of $3,000. Ten years later, total income—keeping pace with inflation of 2 percent per year—has risen to $3,660. At that point, housing costs are 19.2 percent of income.

The renter suffers due to inflation, while the homeowner benefits. So the inflation argument is a strong one in support of investing in your own home. Inflation factors for buying power and cost are shown in Figure 2–3.

Here is where the myth comes into effect. Because fixed-rate housing payments protect you against inflation, so the argument goes, you are secure with the mortgage payments you make. There's no need to change the repayment term.

In fact, the argument is completely wrong. The value of buying rather than renting is widely accepted and true. But we still come back to the question of total cost—the rate of equity buildup and the comparison between homeowner profits and lender profits. The two issues are completely separate.

Mortgage acceleration makes sense, even with a fixed cost of housing, when you consider the actual cost of buying versus the reduction in that cost through acceleration. Using the inflation argument, compare housing values to interest costs.

Example. Again, assuming that annual inflation is 2 percent, the total rate of cost per dollar (Fig. 2–3) in 30 years is $1.81. That means that if housing values keep pace with inflation, your $100,000 house will be worth $181,000 in 30 years. At the same

	buying power of one dollar			
year	1%	2%	3%	4%
0	$1.00	$1.00	$1.00	$1.00
5	.95	.90	.86	.82
10	.90	.82	.74	.66
15	.86	.74	.63	.54
20	.82	.67	.54	.44
25	.78	.60	.47	.36
30	.74	.55	.40	.29

	cost per one dollar			
year	1%	2%	3%	4%
0	$1.00	$1.00	$1.00	$1.00
5	1.05	1.10	1.16	1.22
10	1.10	1.22	1.34	1.48
15	1.16	1.35	1.56	1.80
20	1.22	1.49	1.81	2.19
25	1.28	1.64	2.09	2.67
30	1.35	1.81	2.43	3.24

Figure 2–3 Inflation factor

time, an $80,000 mortgage (after a 20 percent down payment) at 10 percent interest will cost you $252,742 in 30 years. Your housing costs will have exceeded the rate of inflation by more than $70,000.

To *match* your total housing costs, real estate values will have to climb by more than 3 percent per year, or at a rate equal to 150 percent of inflation. Historically, housing values have outpaced inflation, but by nowhere near that rate. And even if values did increase to match your interest costs, it means only that you would break even. The value of your home after inflation would be identical to its purchase price, and you would have no real profits.

A "profit" on a real estate investment is difficult to attain without acceleration of payments in some form. Even though a fixed rate of interest protects you and punishes the renter, when you sell your home and then buy another, inflation will affect both prices. You will receive more for your home, but you also will have to pay more for a new home. The solution: building more equity more rapidly, so that you have more money available to reinvest. That's the only way you really profit from investing in your home.

COMPARING ACCELERATION AND INVESTING

The inflation argument is flawed when used incompletely. If you accept the premise that buying a home fixes your costs and is preferable to renting but ignore the fact that interest erodes your profits, then you have considered only half of the picture.

At certain times in the past, inflation did occur at a very high rate. In instances where the inflation rate is higher than the rate you're paying on your mortgage, acceleration is not a smart idea. As inflation increases, so does the available rate on other investments. For example, if you have a fixed-rate mortgage at 10 percent and you can earn 15 percent in a relatively safe investment (such as a money market mutual fund), then it makes sense to invest money on the outside.

Those circumstances are rare, however, and temporary. Interest rates vary just as other economic factors do and are subject to change. Following the high inflation of the late 1970s and early 1980s the rate fell dramatically. As long as inflation is lower than the rate you're paying on your mortgage, acceleration is a more profitable alternative.

In considering investments, you probably look at two important features—the rate of return and the degree of risk. This method of evaluation should be applied to acceleration, too.

When you reduce interest costs, you *save* money because you will pay less interest. This saving is a form of yield, just as the rate you're paid for opening a savings account is a form of yield. The difference is that with acceleration, you reduce costs, and with a savings account, you increase the value of the money left on deposit.

In either event, the result is the same. Either your money appreciates due to compound interest, or the total amount you must spend is reduced for the same reason. Your monthly mortgage payment is broken down between principal and interest, with the interest computed on the basis of the current loan balance. Every additional payment made today will reduce the interest on *all* future payments. The benefits of acceleration are compounded, just as the money in a savings account is compounded when left on deposit.

Besides the actual yield, you will have a difficult time finding an outside investment as safe as building equity in your own home. You should have a sum available for emergencies, in a savings account or comparably liquid investment. Once that reserve has been established, you might seek additional investments. But to match the savings on your mortgage by accelerating payments, you probably will have to assume a greater degree of risk.

Compare the benefits of saving $100 per month in an insured savings account to putting $100 per month into accelerating your mortgage payments. After 30 years, the savings account will accumulate $64,451 in interest (assuming monthly compounding). However, the same $100 per month added to a 30-year mortgage at 10 percent will *save* $80,798 in total interest. See Figure 2–4.

An additional benefit in increasing payments on your mortgage by $100 per month is that you will completely eliminate the debt in less than 18 years. This method reduces your risk by taking 12 years off the term of repayment, building equity more rapidly, and easing your family's monthly budget.

In the event you need to borrow money later, more rapid equity buildup makes a greater sum available. By accelerating your mortgage, you increase the collateral in your home, giving you greater borrowing power more rapidly. While acceleration reduces the cost of housing, equity can also be viewed as a source for future financing. And the more equity you have, the higher the sum that's available for borrowing in the future.

end of year	yield from $100 per month 6% savings	10% mortgage
5	$ 977	$ 1,744
10	4,388	8,484
15	11,082	23,447
20	22,204	49,681
25	39,299	71,720
30	64,451	80,798

Figure 2–4 Savings and acceleration

SUMMARIZING THE MYTHS

The home-buying public lives with the four common myths about the real cost of housing, the way that equity builds, the value of tax deductions, and the effects of inflation. To summarize these myths:

Myth 1. The purchase price is what you pay for your home.

Problem. In reality, you pay much more than the stated purchase price, because of the interest cost. An $80,000 mortgage at 10 percent over 30 years costs $172,735 in interest—plus the $80,000.

Solution. You have the power to directly control and predetermine the total cost of your home. By beginning a plan for the systematic reduction of interest over time, you can decide on the total repayment date and total purchase price.

Myth 2. Equity is built primarily from increases in market value, due to demand for housing.

Problem. Increased demand is only one of the factors that determines future value. Chances are, the interest you pay to a lender will offset that market demand. As a result, you make much less profit from buying a home than the lender makes.

Solution. By investing in equity, you gain the benefit of compounded interest through reduced costs. In this way, the equity that *you* create can exceed the long-term effects of changing market value.

Myth 3. Acceleration is a poor idea because it reduces the benefits of deducting interest on your tax return.

Problem. Paying full interest means a higher cost for your home, even on an after-tax basis.

Solution. You do reduce itemized deductions by accelerating, but this reduction is offset by greater savings in overall costs. Even after the reduced deductions, you will be much farther ahead with acceleration.

Myth 4. A fixed-rate mortgage protects you from inflation, so that acceleration is unwise and unnecessary.

Problem. This argument is valid when comparing the value of buying to that of renting. But when used to argue against acceleration, it is misleading.

Solution. Recognize the value of fixed housing costs over time, notably as your family's income grows. However, don't ignore the significant savings that are possible from acceleration. Evaluate the acceleration program in comparison to other outside investments.

Before deciding on any course of action, you should gather all your facts. Question common beliefs and myths. Only in this way will you be able to make a completely informed decision. Once you understand the common myths about the cost of buying and paying for your home, you are better prepared to choose a plan that makes sense and works within your budget.

In the next chapter, you will see how loans are paid down over time, how interest is figured each month, and how an active plan for acceleration can yield substantial savings for you.

3 FIGURING LOAN AMORTIZATION

You lose most of your mortgage payments to interest during the earlier years of your mortgage term. Loan balances decline so slowly because the amount of interest is figured based on the amount of loan still unpaid.

When your loan balance is high, more of your payment must go to interest, with only a small amount paid toward the loan itself. So on a mortgage of $80,000, at 10 percent interest, it takes $702.06 every month—for 360 months—to completely pay off that loan. In the first month, $666.67 is for interest, and only $35.39 is applied toward the debt. And that ratio changes very gradually, by only about $0.30 per month at the beginning.

THE GRADUAL SHIFT

The best way to understand the value of acceleration and the high cost of financing your home is to track a 30-year mortgage and to see how painfully slowly that loan is paid off.

You know your payment is $702.06 per month (based on our example of an $80,000 loan at 10 percent, to be paid over 30 years). On *average*, the payment is divided between interest and principal as

Principal	$222.22
Interest	479.84
Total	$702.06

Allowing for rounding, you can prove this average relationship by multiplying the average principal by the number of payments in 30 years:

$$\$222.22 \times 360 \text{ months} = \$79{,}999.20$$

So on average, less than one-third of the total payment goes toward paying off the loan and building equity, while the rest is the cost of borrowing money. But because interest is figured on the outstanding balance, the interest cost in the earlier years of your mortgage term is much greater than it is later on.

For example, while the first month's interest is $666.67, the amount of interest in the 350th month (during the last year of the term) is only $61.20. By that time, $640.86 of your payment goes toward principal.

The gradual swing from high interest payments in the early years to higher principal payments during the later years is significant. And it points out the advantage of acceleration: The sooner you begin a program for additional payments on your mortgage, the lower your overall cost.

The problem, though, for most people buying their first home, is that they simply cannot afford to put more money into their mortgage payment. Indeed, in many cases, they can barely afford the long-term payment itself, even with two working spouses. So how can you afford to accelerate your mortgage?

The answer to that dilemma is that an acceleration program can be started at any time. The earlier you start, the greater the benefit, but the program must be practical, and it must work within the restrictions of your family's budget.

Example. You have owned your home for five years and have built up a comfortable emergency reserve in a money market mutual fund. You now have enough flexibility in your budget to invest $100 per month. In evaluating different investments, you include acceleration as a possibility. What is the value of paying an extra $100 per month toward principal?

To evaluate the investment value of acceleration, you must realize that reducing a 10 percent loan is the equivalent of *earning*

10 percent somewhere else. For every $100 you reduce your loan balance today, you will earn 10 percent for the remainder of your loan term, through reducing the cost of repayment.

By assuming monthly compounding of interest (in the same manner that your mortgage interest is calculated), a $100 payment (at 10 percent) yields (or saves) $1,984 in interest over 30 years. If you have owned your home for five years—meaning you have 25 years to go on your mortgage—every $100 will yield (or save) $1,206.

The value of prepaying $100 is shown at various interest rates in Figure 3–1.

Consider how this applies on an $80,000 loan at 10 percent. If, along with the very first payment, you add $100, you reduce total interest costs over the 30-year term by $1,984, or nearly the equivalent of three monthly payments.

BREAKING DOWN THE PAYMENT

The gradual shift between interest and principal is an expensive problem if you continue making only the required monthly payment. It can also be an opportunity if you recognize the value of compounding and how that relates to prepayments you make today.

A one-time payment benefits you not only by lower interest in the following month but for *every* month remaining in your mortgage term. Interest is reduced because the principal balance is lower by $100 for every future month. Each time you make a

	MORTGAGE INTEREST RATE			
YEARS	8%	10%	12%	14%
5	$ 149	$ 165	$ 182	$ 201
10	222	271	330	402
15	331	445	600	807
20	493	733	1,089	1,618
25	734	1,206	1,979	3,245
30	1,094	1,984	3,595	6,508

Figure 3–1 Value of $100 prepayment

t, interest will be computed on $100 less, because the principal is lower. The benefit is compounded.

Monthly compounding is figured by applying 1/12th of the annual interest rate against the current balance. So with an annual rate of 10 percent, each month's rate is actually .833 percent (1/12th of 10 percent).

The steps for breaking down your monthly payment on a 10 percent loan with $80,000 due are

1. Compute the monthly rate by dividing the annual interest rate by 12 (for the number of months in the year).

Example. .10 (or 10 percent), divided by 12, equals .00833, the monthly rate.

2. Figure out this month's interest by multiplying the monthly rate in step 1 by the amount of the loan still outstanding.

Example. For the first month's payment, the monthly rate of .00833, times the balance of $80,000.00, equals $666.67. That's the amount of the first payment that goes to interest.

3. Subtract the interest figured in step 2 from the total payment made this month to figure the amount of the payment that goes to principal.

Example. Your total payment is $702.06. That total, less the $666.67 figured in step 2, equals $35.39. This amount is the principal payment.

4. Reduce the loan balance by substracting the principal payment.

Example. The loan balance of $80,000.00 at the beginning of the month, less the $35.39 figured in step 3 equals $79,964.61—your new balance.

This process is continued for 360 months, with the amount going to principal gradually increasing. The steps in breaking down your monthly payment are summarized in Figure 3–2.

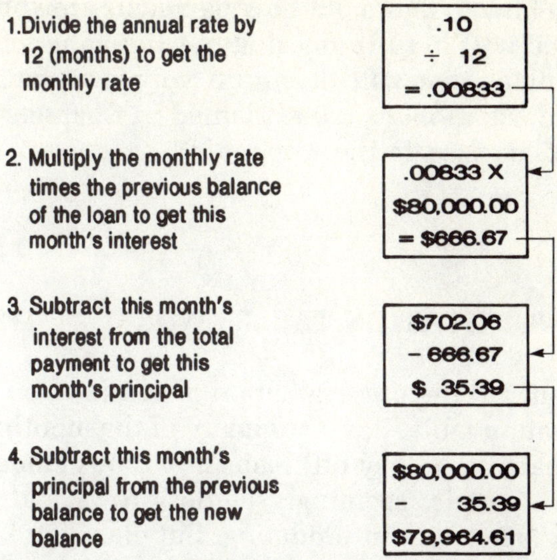

Figure 3–2 Breaking down the monthly payment

The following table shows how payments on an $80,000, 10 percent loan are broken down for the first full year:

Amortizing the Loan

Month	Total Payment	Interest	Principal	Loan Balance
				$80,000.00
1	$ 702.06	$ 666.67	$ 35.39	79,964.61
2	702.06	666.37	35.69	79,928.92
3	702.06	666.07	35.99	79,892.93
4	702.06	665.77	36.29	79,856.64
5	702.06	665.47	36.59	79,820.05
6	702.06	665.17	36.89	79,783.16
7	702.06	664.86	37.20	79,745.96
8	702.06	664.55	37.51	79,708.45
9	702.06	664.24	37.82	79,670.63
10	702.06	663.92	38.14	79,632.49
11	702.06	663.60	38.46	79,594.03
12	702.06	663.28	38.78	79,555.25
Total	$8,424.72	$7,979.97	$444.75	

Knowing how to figure out how payments are applied to your loan balance will help in figuring out the value of various acceleration plans that will fit within your own budget. Several examples of actual plans are explained in Chapters 4 through 6 and are summarized in the Appendix 3.

HOW AMORTIZATION TABLES WORK

An important aid in your evaluation of acceleration programs is the amortization table. It is a summary of the monthly payments required to amortize (pay off) loans of various amounts.

For many people, seemingly endless rows and columns of numbers or factors are intimidating. But once you know how to use the table, it will become clear. You will also discover that being able to read the tables will help you with preplanning and judging the value of a plan to reduce your housing costs.

Every amortization table contains five important elements:

Interest rate, usually printed at the upper right-hand corner of the page

Compounding method (monthly, quarterly, semiannually, or annually), shown in the top middle of the page

Term, the number of years you are given to pay off the loan, listed as headings of a series of columns

Loan amount, listed down the left side in the first column

Monthly payments, the body of the table

Once you locate the correct table to use (10 percent, for example), simply find the correct column (for the years you have to pay your loan) and the right row (for the the loan amount). The figure listed in that column and row is the monthly payment you must make.

An example of a monthly, 10 percent amortization table is shown in Figure 3–3. By going to the row showing the amount of $80,000 and then moving over to the 30-year column, you will see the amount 702.06 listed. This amount is what must be paid each month to completely amortize your loan.

A basic principle of interest is as follows: By increasing the amount paid to principal, the total years required to pay off that loan are also reduced. To judge the value of even a modest acceleration plan, use the amortization table.

Example. What must you do to pay off your 30-year loan in 25 years, and how much will that save?

On the same line you checked for the 30-year payment schedule, Figure 3–3 shows repayment amounts for 15, 20, and 25 years. By checking the monthly payment for a 25-year term, you see that $726.97 is listed. So if instead of paying $702.06 per month, you increase your payment by $24.91 per month, you will pay off your loan five years sooner than planned.

compounding method
interest rate
years to repay the loan
loan amount
monthly payment

MONTHLY 10.00%

PAYMENT REQUIRED TO AMORTIZE A LOAN

TERM	15 YEARS	20 YEARS	25 YEARS	30 YEARS
AMOUNT				
55000	591.04	530.77	499.79	482.67
60000	644.77	579.02	545.23	526.55
65000	698.50	627.27	590.66	570.43
70000	752.23	675.52	636.10	614.31
75000	805.96	723.77	681.53	658.18
80000	859.69	772.02	726.97	702.06
85000	913.42	820.27	772.40	745.94
90000	967.15	868.52	817.84	789.82
95000	1020.88	916.78	863.27	833.70
100000	1074.61	965.03	908.71	877.58

Figure 3–3 Loan amortization table

To figure out the savings, compare the cost of paying over 30 years to that of paying a higher amount over 25 years:

$702.06 × 360 months = $252,741.60
$726.97 × 300 months = $218,091.00
Savings = $34,650.60

By increasing your payment by $24.91 per month, your loan is paid off in fewer years, and you will save more than $34,000 in interest.

You can apply the same test to a repayment term of any number of years, coordinating three essential elements of your plan:

The amount of additional payment you can afford to make, as defined by your family's budget

The number of years in which you would like to repay your loan

The comparison of benefits in acceleration to the potential for profit from other investments

Books of loan amortization tables can be purchased in any bookstore, averaging $5.00. Or you can use the tables listed in the Appendix 1 of this book to test your own plan. The amortization table is a valuable tool in deciding how acceleration will benefit you and in tailoring a plan to fit your own financial requirements. You will be able to estimate the number of years it will take to pay off your loan, even when you add a rounded amount to your monthly payments.

Example. You plan to add $100 to your monthly payment, increasing it from $702.06 to $802.06 per month. How long will it take to pay off your loan?

The sample in Figure 3–3 shows rates only for every five years. In an actual amortization book, the years in between are listed as well. Based on an $80,000 loan at 10 percent, the monthly payments for 17 and for 18 years are

17 years	18 years
816.97	799.88

From this table, you can quickly conclude that a payment of $802.06 will completely pay off your loan in approximately 17½ years.

The amortization table can also be used to estimate the payoff in years when your original loan has already been paid down.

Example. You have owned your home for 12 years and are making payments on a 30-year term. The original loan balance was $80,000, and interest is 10 percent. By checking your latest statement from the lender, you see that your current loan balance is $70,216. What will be the results of amortization?

To estimate the answer, calculate your remaining payments based on the years remaining in your loan term and the current balance. You owe about $70,000, and you have 18 years left in your original mortgage term. A study of an amortization table will reveal that the payment required to pay off a balance of $70,000 in 18 years is the same as that required to pay off a balance of $80,000 in 30 years. In other words, at any point in your mortgage, the current balance, amortized over the remaining term of years, will be about the same as the full-term payment you're already making. This fact is the key to determining how to put an acceleration plan in effect at any time.

Take these steps to calculate the effects of an acceleration program:

1. Using the same 10 percent table, find the line for $70,000 and the row for 18 years. The amortization rate is $699.90. This amount is close to the payment you're actually making, $702.06 per month. The fact that this amount is not exactly the same as your actual payment is not cause for concern. Remember, you are only estimating at this point to determine the results of a lump-sum addition to principal.

2. Compute the effects of adding $100 per month to your cur-

rent payment by looking for the payment on the $70,000 line that is approximately $800 per month. You will find in the column for 13 years the required monthly payment to amortize a $70,000 loan is $803.50 per month.

3. From this information, you can conclude that adding $100 per month starting at the end of your 12th mortgage year reduces the remaining 18-year term to 13 years.

You'll recall an earlier example in which the original loan of $80,000 could be reduced by five years with an increase in the monthly payment of about $24.91 per month. That example demonstrates the advantage of starting an acceleration program as early as possible. To reduce your payment term by five years, you need to add

$24.91 to each payment, starting in the first year, or

about $100 to each payment, starting after the 12th year.

To further compare these two plans for reducing your loan term by five years, estimate the savings (the results are estimates, because the benefits of starting your acceleration plan were based on the approximate payment at the current $70,000 balance):

1. Full amortization, 30 years:

$$\$702.06 \times 360 \text{ months} = \$252,742$$

2. Adding $24.91 during the first year: payments, 300 months:

$$\$726.97 \times 300 \text{ months} = \$218,091$$

3. Adding $100 after the 12th year:
   a. Payments, years 1 to 12:

$$\$702 \times 144 \text{ months} = \$101,088$$

b. Payments, years 13 to 25:

$800 × 156 months = $124,800

c. Total cost = $225,888

By beginning a relatively modest acceleration plan in the first year, this example reveals a total savings of $34,651 ($252,742 less $218,091). In achieving the same final repayment date of 25 years but beginning an acceleration plan after the 12th year, the savings are $26,854 ($252,742 less $225,888). So an earlier acceleration plan is less expensive, and it saves $7,797 more than achieving the same repayment date but starting the plan 12 years later.

ANOTHER TYPE OF TABLE

The interest amortization table described in the preceding pages is fairly easy to use but is not very flexible. Most tables list loan amounts of $50, $100, $500, and $1,000; further amounts at $1,000 intervals up to $50,000; and, finally, further amounts at $5,000 intervals up to $100,000.

As long as you borrow an amount of money equal to one of the amounts shown on the table, you will have no problem finding the amount of your monthly payment. But what if your loan starts out at a balance of $82,550? In this case, you will have to add together the monthly repayment amounts for each segment of the total found on the table.

Example. At 10 percent and over a 30-year term, the monthly payment for an $82,550 loan is

	Amount	Payment
	$80,000	$702.06
	2,000	17.56
	500	4.39
	50	.44
Total	$82,550	$724.45

This calculation is inconvenient and time-consuming, especially if you want to evaluate the value of various acceleration ideas. For this reason, you might find it easier to use a different type of amortization table: one that reports the *factor* rather than the amount.

Note how the required payment listed above, compared to the loan amount, is consistently the same factor. Divide the monthly payment by the loan amount, and, allowing for rounding, you will arrive at the same factor for each segment of the total:

	Amount	Payment	Factor
	$80,000	$702.06	.0087757
	2,000	17.56	.00878
	500	4.39	.00878
	50	.44	.0088
Total	$82,550	$724.45	

Factor tables are constructed with this point in mind. The factor listed on the table is the partial payment (monthly payment) required to amortize "1" (one dollar). When you multiply that factor by the amount of your loan, it will reveal the monthly payment, regardless of the actual loan amount:

$$.0087757 \times \$80,000 = \$702.06$$
$$.0087757 \times \$82,550 = \$724.43$$

The minor difference between the factor result and the previous result is caused by rounding.

A factor table looks like the following example of a 10 percent, monthly compounding amortization schedule:

Years	10%
5	.0212471
10	.0132151
15	.0107461
20	.0965022
25	.0908701
30	.0087758

An actual table will list each and every year, not just increments of five years. To use the factors, simply multiply by the loan amount. You already know that by paying over 30 years you must pay $702.06 per month. This amount was shown in the number table and can also be proven by using the factor:

$$\$80{,}000 \times .0087758 = \$702.06$$

The next question is: What benefit will be derived from paying over a shorter term—20 or 25 years, for example? Looking at the table, you see that the 25-year repayment factor is .0908701 and that the 20-year repayment factor is .0965022. By multiplying these factors times your loan amount, you will find the same answer as that found on the amount tables.

Remember that, whether you use an amount from a table or multiply by a factor, you are dealing with the same questions and will end up with the same answers. The factors are the amounts per dollar, meaning you will have a shorter route to finding the full amount when your loan balance is an odd amount.

CALCULATING REPAYMENT TERMS

You can use either type of amortization table to calculate the effects of different acceleration plans. These calculations can be based either on a target repayment term, or an an additional amount to be paid each month, or a combination of both.

The first type of estimate is constructed by simply comparing the listed rates for your loan amount and then calculating the savings. For $80,000 at 10 percent, for example, we have

Years	Monthly Payment	Extra Payment	Total Payments	Total Saved
30	$702.06	$ —	$252,742	$ —
25	726.97	24.91	218,091	34,651
20	772.02	69.96	185,285	67,457
15	859.69	157.63	154,744	97,998

With this series of calculations, you are now able to judge the relative value of accelerating at different rates. You would like to pay off your loan in 15 years, but can you afford to increase your payments by $157.63 per month? And even if you can afford the extra payment, is the savings of $97,998 justification enough for putting the plan into action? Perhaps the 20-year plan is more practical. You'll save $67,457 and knock off 10 years from the repayment term—for an added payment of $69.96 per month.

This comparative method is most helpful in evaluating how to proceed with an acceleration plan, both in terms of the cost/savings that are possible and in consideration of your family's budget.

The second method is to assume what would happen if you increased the monthly payment by a round amount. For example, note the following:

Extra Payment	Years to Repayment	Total Payments	Total Saved
$ 0	30	$252,742	$ —
100	18	173,232	79,510
200	13½	146,124	106,618
300	11	132,264	120,478

Keeping in mind that the total saved is an estimate (because you are estimating total payoff based on approximate payment levels on the amortization tables), you now have a fairly accurate summary of how acceleration will work.

It will be very desirable to pay off your 30-year mortgage in only 11 years, which would save $120,478 in interest. But you might have to reject this idea, because you simply cannot afford to pay $1,002 per month ($702 plus $300). The alternative plans offer lower savings but might be more practical for you. For example, by adding $100 per month, the savings are $79,510, and the loan will be repaid in about 18 years.

No financial decision can be made intelligently when evaluated in isolation. The value of comparison cannot be understated. There are no grounds for advocating or rejecting a course of action universally. Just as it would be inaccurate to claim that acceleration is a smart plan for everyone, it is equally wrong to state that it is a poor idea in all cases.

Comparing various plans—including not accelerating at all—is the best way to determine value. You must develop a plan in consideration of your budget, in comparison to what you can earn with other investments, and in light of how quickly you would like to pay off your loan.

Example. If your budget today simply cannot afford an additional payment of $100 per month, then an acceleration plan at that level is not practical. And even if you can afford to add $25 per month, you must first establish a more liquid (available) savings fund, so that you will have cash available in case you need it.

Example. If your current mortgage rate is 7 percent and you can earn 10 percent elsewhere, acceleration is not the best-yielding choice. However, you must also compare risks. To earn 10 percent, how much more risk are you willing to assume? Remember that building equity in your own home is one of the lowest-risk investments you can make. If you opt for a higher potential yield elsewhere, be sure you know and can accept whatever extra risks go along with the plan.

Example. If you would like to pay off your loan in 20 years instead of 30, you will have to make a higher payment each month on your mortgage. By coordinating the two considerations—family budget versus desirable repayment date—you can reach a compromise. You might discover that rather than a 20-year repayment term, you might have to settle for 22 or 23 years, just to make the plan affordable within your current budget.

The next chapter discusses the benefits and problems of shorter-term mortgages. For a higher payment, you can save a considerable amount in interest, and might even be able to negotiate a lower rate. But you also will give up the flexibility that comes from creating your own plan based on a full-term mortgage.

4 SHORTER-TERM MORTGAGES

If we compare the costs between a 15-year term and a 30-year term, the substantial savings possible through acceleration will become clear. But the higher monthly payment this plan will involve is simply beyond the budget of many house buyers. Acceleration will be practical only if the plan is designed to fit within the limits of what you can afford.

In this chapter, you will see how a shorter-term mortgage reduces the cost of your home while enabling you to eliminate debt in half the time. We will also see how to solve the budget problem.

THE DECLINE OF MORTGAGE BALANCES

The balance on a 30-year fixed-rate mortgage loan falls extremely slowly during the early years. For example, at a 10 percent rate, you have paid off only 3.4 percent of the total loan after five years of payments. Starting with an $80,000 balance, that means

1. The total of payments in five years is $42,123.60—more than half the amount borrowed.
2. Only $2,740.77 of the total has gone to principal. The balance, $39,382.83, was for interest.

You can save a huge amount of money by paying your loan over 15 years rather than 30. And although the term is cut in half, you need to increase your monthly payment by only 22 percent (from $702.06 per month for 30-year amortization to $859.69 per month).

The percentages of remaining balances on the 30-year and 15-year terms show how the loan falls. Figure 4–1 shows the remaining balances for a 10 percent loan, both for 15 and 30 years.

At the 30-year rate, you have paid off only one-half of your total debt in the 24th year. The other half is paid during the last 6 years of the term. But with a 15-year loan term, you achieve the same level of repayment early in the 11th year.

The shorter-term mortgage gives you the following three advantages.

Lower Interest Cost. Although monthly payments are higher, you will save nearly $98,000 in total interest.

A higher portion of each month's payment is applied toward principal, so the balance declines more rapidly. For example, in the very first month, the portion applied to principal and to interest is

1. 30-year term:

Principal	$ 35.39
Interest	666.67

2. 15-year term:

Principal	$193.02
Interest	666.67

10% REMAINING BALANCE		
END OF YEAR	30 YEARS	15 YEARS
5	96.6%	81.3%
10	90.9	50.6
15	81.7	0
20	66.4	
25	41.3	
30	0	

Figure 4–1 Remaining balances

Compare the difference a few years later. For example, at the beginning of the ninth year, the remaining balance on the 30-year term is $74,826; on the 15-year term, the balance is down to $51,784. At this point, the payment breaks down as

1. 30-year term:

Principal	$ 78.51
Interest	623.55

2. 15-year term:

Principal	$428.16
Interest	431.53

Not only is there a difference in loan balances of more than $23,000; more than half of the 15-year payment from this point forward is assigned to principal. In the 30-year term, most of the monthly payment is still paid to interest.

Faster Payoff. The loan will be repaid in 15 years instead of 30. That means the burden on your family's budget will be relieved sooner, an important consideration for families that are anticipating future costs (such as the college education of their children).

Figure 4–2 shows how very differently your mortgage balance declines over the repayment term for both repayment plans. A 30-year loan's balance falls predominantly during the last 10 years, while the 15-year term enables you to eliminate the same debt in half the time.

Rapid Equity Growth. Because equity in your home is built much more quickly with a shorter-term mortgage, you will own your home free and clear many years sooner. And in the event that you will need to refinance or borrow in the future, more equity means greater secured borrowing power. For example, if you decide later to add on to your home, a shorter-term mortgage gives you more equity, meaning you will be able to borrow more money in the future.

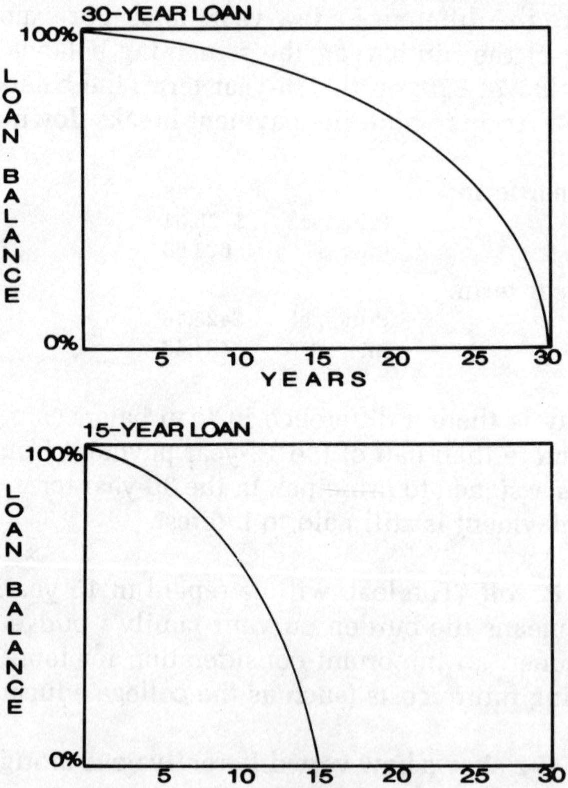

Figure 4–2 Shorter-term repayment

A COST COMPARISON

Achieving a lower overall cost of buying your home through acceleration gives you flexibility, in several ways:

1. When you sell your present home, you will have built a higher amount of equity, meaning more cash to reinvest in another home. For example, if you stay in your present home for 10 years, you will build up equity of only $7,250 on a 30-year term; with a 15-year repayment schedule, your equity will be $39,539.84.

2. The requirement for making mortgage payments is over more quickly. While 15-year payments are higher, you will enjoy greater freedom in your budget at the end of that term.

3. You will gain future borrowing power more rapidly. As your equity increases, so will your ability to finance improvements or to borrow money for any other reason.

4. Your family will have greater security. Remember that the degree of equity you have in your home can and should be equated with financial security. Owing money to a lender is a very real form of risk. The sooner you are able to eliminate that debt, the less risk you carry.

Compare the relative costs of 30-year and 15-year loans, as shown in Figure 4–3. The first two dollar columns show how principal payments build over the loan terms. By the time a 15-year loan is completely paid off, the equity in a 30-year loan is only $14,669.63. Even after only five years, the difference in equity is significant. Most first-time home buyers sell their homes in about five years, so the 15-year equity buildup is an important feature to keep in mind. That's more money to put into your next home. The third and fourth dollar columns show the interest costs at the end of each fifth year. The cost of the 30-year mortgage outpaces the 15-year term by more than the amount of the original loan.

The ever-appreciating value of real estate may offset the interest cost entirely, even without any form of acceleration. Even

	$80,000 LOAN AT 10%			
THROUGH	PAID TO PRINCIPAL		PAID TO INTEREST	
YEAR	30-YEAR	15-YEAR	30-YEAR	15-YEAR
5	$ 2,740.77	$14,947.14	$39,382.83	$36,634.26
10	7,250.24	39,539.84	76,996.96	63,622.96
15	14,669.63	80,000.00	111,701.17	74,743.98
20	26,876.85		141,617.55	
25	46,961.52		163,656.48	
30	80,000.00		172,734.66	

Figure 4–3 Comparing costs

if that is true, however, you will still profit from reducing interest costs. To compare, assume your $100,000 home will increase in value over the next 30 years to a value of $300,000:

	30 Years	15 Years
Appreciated value	$300,000	$300,000
Original cost	$100,000	$100,000
Plus: Interest cost	172,735	74,744
Total cost	$272,735	$174,744
Profit	$ 27,265	$125,256

A common argument against acceleration is that mortgage interest is deductible on your tax return. As the argument goes, you are better off deducting interest than you are accelerating payments. So to make the comparison on an after-tax basis, it is necessary to factor in the tax advantages of deducting interest. Assuming that the effective tax rate is 28 percent each year, the total interest cost in each mortgage term should be reduced by that amount:

	30 Years	15 Years
Total interest paid	$172,735	$ 74,744
Less: 28% tax deduction	48,366	20,928
After-tax interest cost	$124,369	$ 53,816

With the tax benefits of deducting interest in mind, the comparison must be modified to

	30 Years	15 Years
Appreciated value	$300,000	$300,000
Original cost	$100,000	$100,000
Plus: After-tax interest	124,369	53,816
Total cost	$224,369	$153,816
After-tax profit	$ 75,631	$146,184

With the tax benefits in mind, the actual profit from accelerating is reduced from $97,991 (before taxes) to $70,553 (after taxes). On an original investment of $100,000, this difference is still significant, and acceleration makes sense.

AFFORDING EXTRA PAYMENTS

In selecting a loan term, the effect of monthly payments on your budget is a primary concern. Most first-time buyers can barely afford the 30-year payment, and any increase is out of the question.

Another problem is that of qualifying for a loan. Lenders evaluate the risk of granting a mortgage based on your current income and your ability to make monthly payments. So if the required payment is $702 per month, the lender may require that you earn four times that amount, or $2,800. This requirement usually means both spouses must work just to qualify for the loan—and that even the minimum mortgage payment is all the family can afford.

If you want to commit to a 15-year mortgage instead of a 30-year term, the required monthly payment for the same 10 percent loan rises to about $860. Applying the lender's rules for qualification of income equal to four times the payment, your family would have to earn at least $3,440 per month in order to qualify.

The strain on a budget is a major reason that many people take out a 30-year loan, as opposed to a shorter term—even when they are fully aware of the total interest cost.

One advantage of a shorter-term commitment is that lenders will often lower the interest rate. For example, you might be offered a 9¾ percent loan if you agree to repay it over 15 years, instead of a 10 percent loan to be repaid over 30 years.

For the ¼ percent difference, the difference in monthly payment is about $12, based on a 15-year repayment schedule. And, based on an $80,000 loan, total interest cost over the full 15 years (between 9¾ amd 10 percent) is

	Interest
10%	$74,744
9¾%	72,550
Difference	$ 2,194

With this relatively small amount of savings for a ¼ percent difference in the loan rate, you have an advantage by staying with the 30-year mortgage. You can pay off that longer-term loan at the 15-year rate, if you can afford to. If you cannot afford the extra payment, you can revert to the lower monthly required payment whenever you want.

Even if you can qualify with the lender for higher monthly payments, it isn't always smart to commit yourself to a 15-year repayment term. Once you promise to repay at the higher rate every month, you have to make the minimum payment, without exception. An alternative is to commit to a 30-year mortgage and then accelerate that debt according to your family budget.

Think of the slightly higher interest rate as the price you pay for flexibility. When *you* control the repayment term, acceleration is your plan. If you commit to the higher payments with a 15-year term, the strain on your budget could prove too high.

It would be a mistake to commit to a level of payments that you're not sure you could afford. A self-made plan—based on an existing loan with a 30-year term—is more advantageous to you, since you can start and stop whenever you want.

Example. You commit to an $80,000, 30-year mortgage at 10 percent, requiring monthly payments of $702.06. However, you immediately start making payments of $859.69, knowing that this will eliminate the loan in half the time.

Two years later, your monthly living expenses have risen, and you are having difficulty maintaining the higher mortgage payment level. At this point, you have the right to revert to the lower required payment level, or $702.06 per month. You can continue to make only the minimum payment until you can again afford to accelerate.

Your personal financial status changes due to many causes, not all of which you can anticipate: the addition of another child; higher insurance, commuting, food, clothing, and recreation costs; lower than expected raises from your employer; and losing a job. If you are committed to repayments on your mortgage over a 15-year term, it can become a burden to you. By controlling the amount you pay, it's up to you to determine the final cost of your home—but you can also adjust your plan based on changing and unexpected financial burdens in the future.

PICKING YOUR REPAYMENT DATE

You can design a short-term mortgage to specifically suit your own budget. You are not limited only to a choice between 15 and 30 years.

To decide how much acceleration you can afford based on your current budget, compare the cost of paying your mortgage over a number of years. Check a table of amortization payments based on the current balance of your mortgage. At the rate of 10 percent for an $80,000 loan, for example, you will find the following payment levels to pay off your mortgage between 15 and 30 years:

Years	Payment	Years	Payment
15	$859.69	23	$741.74
16	836.72	24	733.91
17	816.97	25	726.96
18	799.87	26	720.78
19	785.01	27	715.28
20	772.02	28	710.37
21	760.62	29	705.98
22	750.60	30	702.06

From this summary, you can easily see the effect of adding varying amounts to your monthly payment. Starting at the 30-year rate of $702.06, you might decide, for example, that you can afford to add $50 per month to your payment, which means the mortgage would be paid off in slightly less than 22 years. Or, you might decide you can afford only about $35 extra per month, so that the mortgage will take 23½ years to eliminate.

Even after establishing a plan for today, you have the right to change it later—as long as you are committed only to the 30-year term. You could completely eliminate the accelerated payment due to temporary financial hardship (maternity leave, losing a job, or unexpected emergencies). You could reduce the acceleration rate to relieve pressure on the budget. Or you could increase the rate of acceleration as your monthly income increases.

Designing your own acceleration plan should include a study

of amortization tables. By tracking the amounts required to pay off a loan over various numbers of years, you will better appreciate the value of adding a few dollars per month to your payment.

A long-term mortgage is permanent (in the sense that you must make payments every month for many years), whereas a self-designed acceleration program is a temporary plan. You select a target represented either by the amount of additional payment or by the desired payoff date. You then change that plan as your personal financial situation changes.

Being able to pick a target date for complete repayment of your mortgage is a valuable feature in your personal financial plan.

Example. You would like to retire in 25 years, but you have 30 years to go until your mortgage is scheduled for repayment. By accelerating at the 25-year rate, you can coordinate mortgage repayment with scheduled retirement dates, thus reducing your monthly retirement income requirement.

Example. You would like to eliminate your mortgage debt before your oldest child graduates from high school, anticipating high college tuition costs. Without the burden of a mortgage payment, you will be able to afford either a new loan or monthly payments to help support your child while in school.

Example. You eventually want to start your own business, but you first want to escape the financial burden of mortgage payments. Acceleration will help you reach this goal sooner. Besides relieving your monthly budget, higher equity also creates the potential for capital you might need in your business.

By remembering that at the time you begin mortgage payments, you might not be able to afford any form of acceleration, there is another way to proceed. As your financial situation improves over the months and years, your mortgage expense is fixed, meaning that it represents an increasingly smaller percentage of your total income. As this change occurs, you can make extra payments toward principal.

The maximum benefit of acceleration is derived by beginning

your plan as early as possible in the mortgage term, when the balance is higher. However, you must also be sure that your plan works. The restrictions of your budget place a limit on how much you can pay, if anything. Even if you cannot afford to make accelerated payments during the first few years you own your home, you can begin adding money to your monthly payment at any time during your repayment term.

Example. You commit to a 30-year, 10 percent mortgage starting with an $80,000 balance. Several years later, your income increases to the point that you can afford more. Based on the current mortgage balance, the amount you can afford, and the year you would like to have that mortgage completely paid off, you can begin a program of acceleration to fit your budget.

Example. You have been paying $702.06 on your 30-year $80,000 mortgage for the last 12 years. The loan's current balance is $70,216. Since you have 18 years to go, check the 10 percent amortization table for 18 years, based on the approximate balance of $70,000. Then review monthly payments required to pay off that balance in fewer years:

Years	Monthly Payment
13	$804
14	776
15	752
16	732
17	715
18	700

Note that the amount required for 18 years—the years remaining in the current term—is about the same as the payment you're now making. It's slightly lower because the comparison is based on a rounded estimate.

From this comparison, you can judge the value of adding to your monthly payment. An extra $50 will cut about three years off the term, and an extra $100 will reduce it by five years.

The rules of flexibility apply in every case. You might begin an acceleration program only to later determine that the level can be raised or that it should be lowered. If you run into unexpected expenses, you can suspend the acceleration plan until your financial situation again improves. And if your income increases, freeing up more cash each month, part of that extra cash can be invested in reducing your mortgage balance more rapidly.

Your acceleration plan is a method for determining the total cost of your home. But for that plan to work, your budget must rule. And you must establish an emergency fund of available cash *before* embarking on a plan of acceleration.

To figure out how much you can afford to prepay, and when the full debt will be eliminated, you can choose from several different acceleration methods. These methods include the preplanned addition of a round amount of money, and the payment of additional principal in an annual lump sum.

In the next chapter we will describe the alternative flexible acceleration plans and their benefits.

5 FLEXIBLE PLANS

As you saw in the last chapter, when you control the degree of acceleration on your mortgage, you allow for unknown circumstances in the future. You can increase, decrease, or even suspend additional payments, all depending on your family budget.

The way to start out with a 30-year term and then design your own plan is preferable to making a commitment to a shorter term. The primary purpose of acceleration is to reduce the true overall cost of buying your home. But the most important consideration in trying to reduce that cost must be what your budget can bear.

This chapter introduces several different acceleration plans, compares the savings they bring about, and explains the advantages of each.

DESIGNING YOUR OWN PLAN

If you are to succeed with an acceleration plan, it must be practical and affordable. Once you invest money in reducing your home's cost, you cannot get it back easily or quickly.

Example. You increase monthly payments in order to accelerate the repayment term. But several months later, an emergency arises, and you need cash. If you had been putting that cash into a savings account or a money market fund, you would be able to get the money at once. However, your mortgage lender will not simply give you the cash you have invested in equity. If you want to get that back, you'll have to borrow money.

The preceding example describes one of the points about an acceleration plan that you must think about before proceeding. When you open a savings account or invest money in the stock market, you have the flexibility of cashing it in. But when you accelerate your mortgage, you're putting more equity into your home. And in one sense, that means the money is permanently invested. The only way you can get it back is to use the higher equity as collateral for another loan.

Too much emphasis is placed on "getting the equity out of your home." You have probably seen ads suggesting that you do just that. But when you get that equity, you are borrowing money, and borrowing is an expensive move. Acceleration ties up your investment cash in your own home, whereas a savings account is available to you on demand.

A subsequent loan will be secured by the equity in your home, but it's still borrowed money. So your acceleration plan should be started only after you conclude that you can afford to tie up your money in the form of equity. Once you're sure you can afford to not have that money available, you should then make additional payments only at the level you can absolutely spare each month or each year. That level will not always be the same as when you begin.

Having taken the precaution of identifying how much you can afford, you will find that the permanent feature of accelerated equity payments will become an advantage. It's only a problem if you extend acceleration beyond a reasonable level. Working the plan into your overall budget (including a reserve of cash for future emergencies) is a form of forced savings. You reduce the cost of your home by paying much less in interest.

Example. Paying over 15 years instead of 30 years results in a savings of $96,991 in interest (based on an $80,000 mortgage). Assuming a 20 percent down payment on a $100,000 home, that means the total cost (over 15 years) is $174,744, rather than the 30-year cost of $272,735:

	30 Years	15 Years
Down payment	$ 20,000	$ 20,000
Amount borrowed	80,000	80,000
Interest	172,735	74,744
Total cost	$272,735	$174,744

If we apply a 28 percent tax rate to both payment methods (to allow for deductible interest), the difference is still substantial:

	30 Years	15 Years
Down payment	$ 20,000	$ 20,000
Amount borrowed	80,000	80,000
After-tax interest	124,369	53,816
Total cost	$224,369	$153,816

Even on an after-tax basis, acceleration in this case reduces the cost of your home by more than $70,000. Varying levels of savings can be achieved with other forms of acceleration, designed to suit your own budget.

BUILDING PAYMENTS INTO YOUR BUDGET

There are two ways to approach acceleration: by building a regular amount of additional payment into your monthly budget and by periodically applying a lump sum to your mortgage.

The first method has the advantage of habit. Most families adjust their life-style to suit available income—which means that as you earn more, you spend more. So when you are required to pay $700 per month on your mortgage but you pay $800, you have created a specific level of monthly expense. As your income rises in the future, the additional monthly payment—because it's already built into your budget—is not a burden.

The second method has its advantages, too. You might not be able to afford adding the same amount to your payment each month, because you simply do not have enough money left over after paying for food, utilities, clothing, insurance, and your other recurring expenses. In addition, when you are able to save even a modest amount of money, an unexpected expense comes along and you end up using what you've saved. However, you might occasionally come into some unexpected funds—an annual bonus or income tax refund, for example.

We will compare six different plans for accelerating your mortgage, all based on an $80,000 loan at 10 percent interest.

Plan 1: Full amortization over 30 years, requiring a monthly payment of $702.06

Plan 2: Amortization over a 15-year term, at the rate of $859.69 per month

Plan 3: Adding $100 per month to your payment, for a total of $802.06 per month

Plan 4: Adding $200 per month to your payment, for a total of $902.06 per month

Plan 5: Adding $1,000 to the first payment you make each year. (During the first month, you pay $1,702.06, and for the other 11 months, you pay the minimum required, $702.06)

Plan 6: Adding $2,000 to the first payment you make each year. (During the first month, you pay $2,702.06, and for the other 11 months, you pay the minimum required, $702.06)

To start out, here's an overview of the results you will achieve with each of the six plans. In all cases of acceleration, you will reduce your repayment term by a number of years:

Plan	Months	
1	360	(30 years)
2	180	(15 years)
3	215	(17 years, 11 months)
4	162	(13 years, 6 months)
5	224	(18 years, 8 months)
6	171	(14 years, 3 months)

The remaining balances of the original loan at the end of each five-year interval reveal the relative speed of acceleration, as shown in Figure 5–1.

	PERCENTAGE OF LOAN OUTSTANDING					
END OF YEAR	PLAN 1	PLAN 2	PLAN 3	PLAN 4	PLAN 5	PLAN 6
5	96.6	81.3	86.9	77.2	88.1	79.7
10	90.9	50.6	65.3	39.7	68.6	46.3
15	81.7	0	29.9	0	36.5	0
20	66.4		0		0	
25	41.3					
30	0					

Figure 5–1 Remaining balances on $80,000 loan at 10% interest. Plan 1—30-year term, $702.06 per month; plan 2—15-year term, $859.69 per month; plan 3—increase payment $100 to $802.06 per month; plan 4—increase payment $200 to $902.06 per month; plan 5—pay $1,000 extra, first month each year; plan 6—pay $2,000 extra first month each year

With this comparison, you can see that the more rapid the acceleration during the earlier years of your mortgage term, the more quickly the loan balance falls—and the more equity you build. Even if you accelerate only during the first five years or so, you will achieve substantial savings from the plan.

Example. In one family, both spouses work at the time they buy their home. However, they also want to have children in a few years. So they agree to the following sequence of events:

1. Both spouses will continue to work for the next five years, and the mortgage will be accelerated at a rate that fits the family budget. At the same time, an amount of money will be placed into a savings account every month.
2. In five years, they will start their family. The wife will quit her job and stay at home until their child is three years old. At this point, the acceleration plan will be suspended.
3. When the wife returns to work, the family will determine whether or not to resume an accelerated repayment schedule.

The preceding example describes the tailoring of a plan not only to suit the family's financial capabilities but to make it flexible enough for future changes. You cannot possibly know what your financial situation will be 5 or 10 years from now, so flexibility is a valuable feature in your financial plan.

AFTER-TAX COMPARISONS

The various acceleration plans you consider should be compared on an after-tax basis. In our examples, we will use a tax rate of 28 percent. However, in your own case, the actual rate will vary, depending on the total of your annual income, the level of itemized deductions you claim, and whether or not you must pay state and local taxes, in addition to federal taxes.

The tax rate is based on taxable income, meaning your total income after reductions for

Adjustments to gross income (for IRA payments, reimbursed business expenses, and alimony payments, for example)

Exemptions claimed

Itemized deductions or the standard deduction

The tax rate you pay is the percentage of taxable, not total, income. The 1987 federal tax tables apply the 28 percent rate for taxable income between $28,000 and $45,000. The amount of tax in this range is $4,050 plus 28 percent of the amount above $28,000.

So, in fact, if your income is exactly $28,000, your tax bill of $4,080 is only 14.6 percent, but anything you earn *above* that amount is subject to the 28 percent additional tax.

Example. As of December 30, your taxable income for the year is exactly $28,000. On the last day of the year, you earn another $1,000. The additional tax on this amount will be $280.

The same rule applies to deductions. The value of a deduction above the base rate is equal to 28 percent of the deduction.

Example. On December 30, your taxable income is $29,000, so your total tax will be $4,360 ($4,080 plus 28 percent of the amount above $28,000). If you are able to come up with an additional $1,000 in deductions before the end of the year, those deductions will reduce your total tax by 28 percent, or $280.

With these computations in mind, it would be inaccurate to assume that any tax rate would apply to your total income. It's computed based on a range of taxable income only.

How does this affect our comparison of different methods of acceleration? Chances are that any tax rate you assume will not be entirely accurate, because you won't know your future level of gross or taxable income or the rate of tax resulting from future federal tax laws. The higher the rate you assume, the less advantage you will gain from accelerating your mortgage payments.

We will use the 28 percent rate as a "worst-case" comparison. If your actual tax rate is lower, then your advantages from acceleration will be greater than those shown.

Example. The savings in a 15-year plan and a 30-year plan vary according to the tax rate you apply in the comparison:

	Interest		
	30 Years	15 Years	Savings
Before taxes	$172,735	$74,744	$97,991
28% tax rate	124,369	53,816	70,553
22% tax rate	134,733	58,300	76,433
15% tax rate	146,825	63,532	83,293

The lower the tax rate you assume, the greater the savings on an after-tax basis.

COMPARING THE PLANS

The first plan—payments without any acceleration—requires 360 payments over 30 years and involves interest of $172,735. That means your $100,000 house will cost you $272,735.

The other five plans reduce the total cost of your home by varying amounts, as summarized in Figure 5–2.

The last column in Figure 5–2 shows the amount saved with each of the plans presented, in comparison to the 30-year sched-

PAYMENT METHOD	TOTAL PAYMENTS	INTEREST PAYMENTS	AMOUNT SAVED
full amortization, 30 years	$252,735	$172,735	$ —
15-year amortization	154,744	74,744	97,991
add $100 per month	171,937	91,937	80,798
add $200 per month	146,027	66,027	106,708
add $1,000 each year	176,238	96,238	76,497
add $2,000 each year	149,671	69,671	103,064

Figure 5–2 Savings comparison

ule. If we stay with the assumption that you will pay taxes at the rate of 28 percent every year throughout the mortgage term, the after-tax savings must be adjusted:

Plan	Before Taxes	28%	After Taxes
30 years	$ —	$ —	$ —
15 years	97,991	27,437	70,554
Add $100 per month	80,798	22,623	58,175
Add $200 per month	106,708	29,878	76,830
Add $1,000 per year	76,497	21,419	55,078
Add $2,000 per year	103,064	28,858	74,206

The common argument against acceleration points out that on an after-tax basis, you *lose* money. With the 15-year plan, for example, you lose $27,437 in deductions over the term of repayment. And you are also required to pay more per month in order to accelerate the mortgage.

What this argument overlooks is the after-tax effect of acceleration. In the process of "losing" $27,437 in deductions, you are also reducing the after-tax savings of $70,554. You are not really losing money at all. You're saving money by reducing the amount of interest paid, even with taxes considered.

Never be swayed by the argument concerning lost tax deductions. It doesn't make sense, regardless of the effective tax rate. Remember instead that the true cost of your home must include the overall cost, which involves interest—at a level you can control to a significant degree.

With the after-tax cost in mind, a $100,000 home will cost about $224,000 if amortized over 30 years (including $124,000 after-tax interest). And at the accelerated 15-year rate, the same home costs about $154,000 after taxes. So the question regarding acceleration, at the 15-year rate, should be the following: Would you rather pay $224,000 or $154,000 for your home?

Another argument involves the lost opportunity of acceleration. The money put into additional equity could be invested elsewhere. While this is true, there are three important points to remember:

1. You might not be able to earn a rate of interest equivalent to what you're paying on your mortgage. And even if you can get a better rate today, it could change in the future. Remember that the mortgage rate applies through the term of the loan. The investment rate you earn will change with different economic conditions.

2. The risk of an outside investment, compared to the risk of acceleration, will almost always be greater. The higher the yield on an outside investment, the greater the risk of loss.

3. Whatever you do earn on other investments will also be taxable, a point often overlooked by the critics of acceleration.

BORROWING POWER AND ACCELERATION

You might hesitate to begin a plan, especially in light of the illiquidity of acceleration. You cannot get that money back without applying for a new loan or additional financing, and the uncertainty of the future could make any form of acceleration a serious risk. The emergency reserve fund that you should establish before starting acceleration will mitigate this problem in most cases. But what if you run into a financial problem you just didn't expect?

Example. You begin what you consider a moderate plan of acceleration and continue it for two years. But then you are fired from your job, and it looks like you'll be out of work for several months. You have an emergency reserve fund, but it probably won't cover all of your current expenses for more than a month or two.

In this case, there are several steps you can take:

1. You should immediately stop accelerating mortgage payments. The immediate problem of staying solvent is more critical than the longer-term savings from reduced interest costs. This is a time to defer expenses as much as possible.
2. You should visit the lender and discuss the problem with a loan officer. Telling your lender exactly what is going on will result in greater cooperation than you can expect if you end up making late payments. You might be able to negotiate a delay in mortgage payments. As long as you've made past payments on time, most lenders will grant a limited deferral—especially if you visit the lender and explain the problem before it really becomes a problem. And the fact that you have been accelerating payments in the past strengthens your case. Because you have higher equity in your home, the lender's risks are lowered.
3. You might be able to use the equity in your home to avoid severe financial problems. In the worst possible situation, you could be forced to sell your home. If that occurs, you will have more cash in hand after the sale.

If you are granted a limited deferral of mortgage payments, you will continue to accrue interest on the outstanding balance. So while payments are suspended, the loan balance will increase each month. But this situation is acceptable, considering that you have accelerated in the past and that you need the time to find other work.

Example. You have been accelerating your 10 percent loan by adding $100 per month over the last nine years. The current balance of the loan is $56,434.25. Your lender grants you a three-month suspension in monthly payments. During that time, the loan balance will increase due to accruals of interest:

Month	Interest	Balance
		$56,434.25
1	$470.29	56,904.54
2	474.20	57,378.74
3	478.16	57,856.90

The loan will have increased by $1,422.65 in three months, rather than declining. But even with this reversal, compare the situation without any acceleration at all: If you had been paying only the amount required to pay off your loan over 30 years, the balance of the loan after nine years would be $73,839.57, or more than $23,000 higher. The lender will probably be less willing to grant you the suspension in this case, but even if it is granted, the three-month cost will be much greater:

Month	Interest	Balance
		$73,839.57
1	$615.33	74,454.90
2	620.46	75,075.36
3	625.63	75,700.99

From the lender's point of view, the limited amount of equity you've built up during nine years make three-month suspension a risky idea. Not only is the loan balance increased by $1,861.42; the amount of debt is dangerously close to the amount of the original loan.

The preceding example demonstrates how acceleration can later work out as a benefit, through strengthening the lender's evaluation of risk. With an acceleration plan, the amount of equity is built up more rapidly, so that the risk to the lender is much lower.

An acceleration plan increases your borrowing power. When you have substantial equity built up in your home, a high credit limit on a charge card, or a line of credit with your bank, you have one or more forms of borrowing power. You achieve this power through rapid acceleration. So even though your accelerated payments are "permanently" invested in your home, most lenders will respond to temporary financial problems with greater flexibility.

CHANGING THE PLAN

A complete summary of the yearly status for each plan of acceleration is shown in Appendix 3, along with annual after-tax interest costs, total cash payments, and yearly remaining balances. These tables assume that you initiate a plan at the beginning of your mortgage term and never alter it.

Some interesting possibilities arise, though, when you consider the benefits and practical applications of changing your plan to suit your financial status and budget. You could decide to alter your plan in one of two ways:

Alternative 1. Increase payments periodically, based on the amount of income you are earning.

One of the greatest benefits in buying a home is that monthly payments are fixed, without even starting an acceleration plan. Over time, that fixed payment represents an ever-decreasing percentage of your total income. This fact applies even with a variable-rate mortgage, assuming the loan agreement includes an interest rate cap (a maximum rate the lender can charge).

This benefit can be turned around and viewed in another way. While a fixed cost is beneficial, it also means your flexibility increases over time. As your mortgage represents a smaller portion of future income, you will have a wider range of acceleration choices. So while you might be able to afford only $25 per month today, you will probably be able to increase the degree of acceleration in the future.

Alternative 2. Decrease or suspend accelerated payments due to unexpected expenses or financial burdens.

If you commit to a 15-year mortgage, you *must* make the required payment each month—assuming you can qualify for the higher payment to begin with. But with a 30-year term, you have the right to increase or decrease your payment, as long as you always pay at least the required amount. So as unexpected events occur, you can suspend or decrease acceleration. This alternative places tremendous flexibility in a budget, even one designed with the forced-savings feature of acceleration.

Example. You begin adding a minimal amount to your monthly payment but later stop because you have expenses to pay. The money you've put into added equity is still there and is still working to reduce the interest payments you continue to make each month. If, as an alternative, you placed the same amount into a savings account, chances are you would withdraw those funds as unexpected expenses came up. Typically most families have difficulty saving money for that reason. Putting cash into a savings account is only half of the goal. The other half is being able to resist the temptation to remove it.

Evaluating the benefits of different plans, based both on your budget and rate of interest, is an individual matter. No two families will conclude that any one plan best suits their needs. This difference is due not only to varying monthly income and expense levels but also to the amount of importance assigned to reducing interest costs and the ultimate price of a home.

The desirability of rapid acceleration is made even more complex when your mortgage comes with a variable rate rather than a fixed rate. We will evaluate the strategies in this situation in the next chapter.

6 PLANS FOR ADJUSTABLE-RATE MORTGAGES

It is fairly straightforward to evaluate the value of a mortgage acceleration plan as long as your interest rate is fixed. But when your loan is established with an adjustable rate, your analysis must be made on an entirely different basis.

On the one hand, any increase above the required monthly payment increases the repayment rate and lowers interest costs. But at the same time, any time the lender increases the interest rate upward, that also increases the amount of interest you pay each month.

In this chapter, you will see how a mortgage acceleration plan can reduce interest costs by more than $100,000, even with an adjustable rate, and how a 30-year repayment term can be cut by 11 years or more.

THE ADJUSTABLE-RATE LOAN

The traditional 30-year fixed-rate term was the standard mortgage until the late 1970s. Then, as a severe inflationary economy drove interest rates up as high as 20 percent and more, lenders discovered that they had a problem. Long-term loans with relatively low fixed rates were yielding less income to the lenders than the going cost of money.

Example. A lender must pay 12 percent to borrow money and then lends it out at a 16 percent rate. The spread (percentage of gross profit) is 4 percent. However, the lender has many existing loans that yield only 7 or 8 percent and that have many years to go before repayment.

Because of this condition, the adjustable-rate loan was devised. In this form of contract, the lender can increase the annual interest rate as the cost of money increases. The degree of increase is tied to an independent outside index that measures interest rates, either nationally or regionally.

Home buyers require long-term financing in order to afford the properties they purchase. And they also need to ensure that future payments will be affordable to them. From the lenders' point of view, either the income from lending money in the long term must be high enough to be acceptable if rates go up in the future, or, preferably, the lenders must have the option of raising their rates.

Lenders adjust the rates on the variable mortgage based on changes in the outside index. As the index rate rises, your adjustable loan rate will be increased to the same degree.

Most adjustable-rate loans place a limit on the maximum possible interest rate that will be assessed during the term of the loan and also on the amount of increase that will be applied each year. These limits are the lifetime cap and yearly cap.

Example. A lender offers an adjustable-rate loan that starts at 8 percent. The terms further include a lifetime cap of 5 percent and an annual cap of 1 percent. Under these terms, the maximum increase the lender may assess is 1 percent per year, to a total increase of 5 percent:

Year	Maximum Rate
1	8%
2	9
3	10
4	11
5	12
6–on	13

Bear in mind that the annual and lifetime caps are the *maximum* rates you will pay on an adjustable-rate loan. If the independent index being used does not increase significantly, the actual interest rate will be lower. And if the index rate falls in a subsequent year, so will the loan rate.

Some forms of adjustable-rate mortgages come with a payment cap instead of a rate cap. These mortgages are not as favorable to you as a borrower. The interest rate could rise substantially above the maximum payment you are guaranteed, so that the payment is not large enough to cover each month's interest. In that case, your loan balance will *rise* each year rather than fall, a condition known as negative amortization (and the opposite of mortgage acceleration).

The rate cap, in comparison, includes a payment cap based on the maximum rate. But a payment cap, by itself, does not allow for the problem of current rates rising far above what's required to amortize the loan.

Example. In an adjustable-rate mortgage for $80,000, starting at 8 percent and involving a five-point cap, the maximum rate is 13 percent. On a 30-year repayment schedule, that caps your payment at $884.96. So with the rate cap, a payment cap already exists.

Payment caps are marketed by some lenders with this argument: You are guaranteed that your monthly payment will never be greater than the payment cap. This argument is reassuring, especially for the buyer who is nervous about the adjustable rate. In that situation, you need reassurance that you'll be able to afford future increases in your monthly payment. But that reassurance is deceptive when you look at what can happen if interest rates go beyond the payment cap level.

Example. You commit to an adjustable-rate mortgage that starts out at 8 percent interest. The loan balance is $80,000, and monthly payments (with a 30-year amortization term) are $587.02. The payment cap is $700, and the lender can adjust your payment every two years. Two years later, your balance has declined to $78,608, and the lender adjusts your rate to 11 percent.

Starting with the third year, the monthly interest (11 percent of $78,608, divided by 12 months) is $720.57—but your payment cap is $700. During the next three months, your payments will be applied as follows:

Payment	Interest	Principal	Balance
			$78,608.00
$700.00	$720.57	$−20.57	78,628.57
700.00	720.76	−20.76	78,649.33
700.00	720.95	−20.95	78,670.28

Notice that the loan balance rises each year, instead of falling. This condition will continue as long as you make only the required maximum payment. The loan balance is rising each month, a condition that any home buyer will certainly agree is unacceptable.

Some lenders also attract borrowers to adjustable-rate loans by offering an extremely low initial rate. But in the fine print of the contract, you will find a clause stating that after six months or one year, that attractive rate is replaced with a much higher one. The initial rate, called the "*teaser*," is written into the agreement to make adjustable-rate loans more attractive than fixed-rate loans, at least initially. Some borrowers might have to go with such loans just to qualify. But if you take a very low-rate mortgage, you must also expect a drastic increase in your monthly payments within a year.

The mistake many buyers make is in shopping for financing. While you want the most favorable terms, the adjustable-rate mortgage with a teaser rate is only a gimmick and will not reduce your overall cost. It will only increase the total price of your home.

ACCELERATING WITH AN ADJUSTABLE RATE

With the basic rules of adjustable-rate mortgages in mind, you can see that the strategies for acceleration must be different. Not only are you interested in reducing the years and total interest cost; you must also plan ahead for increases in the interest rate. At the same time, you must also ensure that the plan you initiate is practical in the context of your monthly budget.

There are two ways to approach acceleration with an adjustable-rate mortgage:

1. Begin a plan of acceleration with a higher than required monthly payment that will remain level throughout the term.
2. Offset interest rate increases with a correspondingly higher monthly payment.

With the first method, you have the advantage of paying down the loan at an initially higher rate than required by contract. But that also requires a monthly payment that might be beyond your budget. For this plan to work, the payment must be adequate to amortize the loan within the term the lender has allowed, even if your interest rate rises to the maximum; the payment must also be affordable now.

With the second method, the rate of loan amortization is controlled, so that your monthly payment increases gradually. This method is more likely to fit your family budget, assuming your income rises over the years that you will be paying on your mortgage. It will not save as much interest as the first plan, but for most people, it is a more practical approach.

For the purpose of comparison, we will make the following assumptions about an adjustable-rate loan:

1. The original loan is for $80,000.
2. The loan terms state that interest starts at 8 percent and that the lender may increase it by no more than 1 percent per year.
3. The loan has a lifetime cap of five points, so that the maximum interest can rise to 13 percent.
4. The maximum increase will be applied each year.

The final assumption—that the maximum increase will be applied each year—is one that you should always make with an adjustable-rate mortgage. If the change in the index being used exceeds the maximum increase the lender can apply, the excess may be held over and applied to later years. So, chances are, your interest rate will rise at the maximum speed allowed by the contract and then will remain at that level for the balance of the term.

The first question you must address is what terms to agree to. For example, will you commit to a 15-year or a 30-year repayment rate?

Some people will argue that while a 30-year term is preferable with a fixed-rate loan, you should take a shorter term for adjustable-rate mortgages. The reasoning is that, with the uncertainty about your future payment, more rapid acceleration is necessary. This argument is valid. However, the maximum payment itself is so much higher with a 15-year term that you could create a severe financial hardship for yourself with a shorter-term loan.

Apply the same argument for an adjustable-rate loan as you do for a fixed-rate loan: Commit to the longer term and then accelerate. Remember that, with a lower minimum monthly payment, you have greater flexibility and control. You can start, stop, increase, and decrease the rate of acceleration based on changing financial circumstances.

By using our assumptions about changing interest rates, the minimum required monthly payments for 15-year and 30-year terms are significantly different. They are shown in Figure 6–1.

YEARS	INTEREST RATE	MONTHLY PAYMENT 15–YEAR	30–YEAR
1	8%	$ 764.53	$ 587.02
2	9	811.42	643.70
3	10	859.69	702.06
4	11	909.28	761.86
5	12	960.14	822.90
6–end	13	1,012.20	884.96

Figure 6–1 Monthly cost of $80,000 adjustable-rate loan (8% with 5-point cap)

At the maximum rate of 13 percent, you are required to make a monthly payment of more than $1,000 under the terms of a 15-year mortgage. However, with the longer 30-year term, the maximum is much lower.

THE LEVEL-PAYMENT PLAN

The first way to approach acceleration with an adjustable-rate loan is by paying the same amount every month. In the example of a 30-year loan of $80,000, the required payment starts out—at the 8 percent rate—at $587.02 per month. What would happen if payments of $885 were made every month? See Figure 6–2.

The interest rate is expected to increase by 1 percent each year. So the rate of amortization declines as the rate changes until the maximum interest rate is reached. However, by the time the sixth year begins, the loan balance has been reduced enough so that the level of $885 per month can be continued.

In this example, you would establish your monthly payments at approximately the same amount required to amortize the loan if it had a fixed rate of 13 percent (the maximum under the terms of this loan). As a result the entire loan will be paid off in about 16 years, and you will save more than $137,000 in interest.

This plan assumes that you can afford to pay $885 each month, or about $300 more than the *required* initial payment. Keep in mind that, with an increasing interest rate, you will ultimately

YEAR	INTEREST RATE	PAYMENT REQUIRED	PAYMENT MADE
1	8%	$587.02	$885.00
2	9	643.70	885.00
3	10	702.06	885.00
4	11	761.86	885.00
5	12	822.90	885.00
6–end	13	884.96	885.00

Figure 6–2 Plan 1: level payments, $80,000 loan, 30-year term

end up paying that amount each month and that the loan would require 30 years to repay without any acceleration. Many people enter loan agreements knowing the payment will rise and hoping that their incomes will increase to offset the higher cost. If you are willing to commit to a 30-year repayment, and if you accept an adjustable rate, the acceleration plan begins to look more reasonable.

A summary of the amortization rate during the first five years follows:

End of Year	Rate	Interest Paid	Principal Paid	Balance
				$80,000.00
1	8%	$6,241.76	$4,378.24	75,621.76
2	9	6,756.02	3,863.98	71,757.78
3	10	7,013.42	3,606.58	68,151.20
4	11	7,334.25	3,285.75	64,865.45
5	12	7,622.21	2,997.79	61,867.66

From this point forward, the interest rate will be fixed at 13 percent (less if the index rate falls). Yet payments will continue at $885 per month, and the loan will be paid off in another 11 years.

In this example, all the acceleration takes place during the first five years—but the benefits of that acceleration take 14 years off the total repayment period. The amount that is applied to principal during these early years declines each year, due to the rising interest rate. Then, once the maximum rate has been reached, the yearly principal portion will begin to increase. At that point, the loan balance will decline in the same way as a fixed-rate mortgage.

This plan is appropriate when you must agree to a variable-rate mortgage just to qualify for financing but you know that you can afford to pay a higher amount.

Example. You and your spouse earn a total of $2,400 per month. When you bought your house, you wanted a fixed-rate loan to finance $80,000, for which the interest rate was 10 percent. The lender would not grant you the loan because your income did not meet its test that total income must be at least four times the monthly payment. A 10 percent loan, paid over 30 years, would require payments of $702.06 per month, so that your gross income would have to be more than $2,800.

The lender proposed an alternative: commit to a 30-year adjustable-rate mortgage starting at 8 percent. The initial monthly payment, $587.02, is within your qualification range. You agree, knowing that you can afford to pay $885 per month. By making payments at that level, you will cut the cost of your home by more than $137,000.

THE PRINCIPAL OFFSET PLAN

If the $885 level is too high for the current budget, the second acceleration plan will be more practical. With this method, you pay the mortgage at a rate slightly above the required amount and adjust it each year, as the interest rate increases.

By assuming the interest rate will increase by 1 percent per year, this plan involves paying at the rate that is 1 percent above what's required. So when the rate is 8 percent, you pay the amount that would be required at 9 percent, and when the rate is 9 percent, you pay the amount that would be required at 10 percent.

This plan has the effect of equalizing both the yearly interest expenses and the payments to principal. It is summarized in Figure 6–3.

When you reach the maximum of 13 percent, you equalize

YEAR	INTEREST RATE	PAYMENT REQUIRED	PAYMENT MADE
1	8%	$587.02	$643.70
2	9	643.70	702.06
3	10	702.06	761.86
4	11	761.86	822.90
5	12	822.90	884.96
6–end	13	884.96	936.31

Figure 6–3 Plan 2: principal offset, $80,000 loan, 30-year term

monthly payments at $936.31 per month. That's about $11 below the amount that would be required at the rate of 14 percent.

Here's how the second plan reduces your mortgage balance during the first five years:

End of Year	Rate	Interest Paid	Principal Paid	Balance
				$80,000.00
1	8%	$6,350.56	$1,373.84	78,626.16
2	9	7,019.31	1,405.41	77,220.75
3	10	7,655.19	1,487.13	75,733.62
4	11	8,250.41	1,624.39	74,109.23
5	12	8,794.89	1,824.63	72,284.60

Beginning with the first payment in the sixth year, the payment is increased to $936.31. That will result in a repayment schedule totaling approximately 19 years.

The first plan presented called for a substantial and immediate cost, while this one involves a gradual increase over a six-year period. That makes the second plan much more practical for most families. As your monthly income rises, you can afford a somewhat higher mortgage payment.

By staying 1 percent ahead of the effective annual interest rate, you will cut 11 years off your mortgage term and save more than $100,000 on the overall cost of your home. This plan also enables you to increase the amount going to principal each year, by offsetting the rise in interest costs.

This plan is an example of an acceleration plan suited to your budget. Rather than imposing too high a rate of acceleration, it is designed to match rising interest over several years. The amount of each year's increase over the required payment level is as follows:

Year	Payment	Amount of Increase	Percent of Increase
1	$643.70	$56.68	9.7%
2	702.06	58.36	9.1
3	761.86	59.80	8.5
4	822.90	61.04	8.0
5	884.96	62.06	7.5
6	936.31	51.35	5.8

While each year's *amount* of increased payment is slightly higher than the year before (through the first five years), the *percentage* of increase declines over the same time. So as long as your income rises steadily through the years you own your home—as most families experience—the portion of your income going toward your mortgage declines.

From the sixth year through the end of the term, the payment is fixed at $936.31 per month. As your total income continues to rise for these remaining years, the portion of the total continues to become lower and lower. So while you have accelerated your mortgage payment and reduced interest by more than $100,000, you are still paying a lower portion of your income toward your mortgage every year.

COMPARING ACCELERATION PLANS

For the adjustable-rate mortgage acceleration plan to work, it must be designed in consideration of your budget. The first plan reduces $33,000 more than the second plan, and repayment occurs three years sooner; however, the gradual increase in monthly payments is probably a more realistic approach for most people.

The two plans are compared to full amortization in Figure 6–4.

Either plan will reduce the total cost of your home by more than $100,000 (given the original loan balance, the range of rates, and the other terms used in our examples). And as with all acceleration plans, the term is reduced well below 30 years by paying more than the lender requires.

	30-YEAR TERM	PLAN 1	PLAN 2
total payments	$307,698	$169,920	$203,086
less: original loan	80,000	80,000	80,000
interest expense	$227,698	$ 89,920	$123,086
years	30	16	19
amount saved		$137,778	$104,612

Figure 6–4 Accelerating with an adjustable rate

These methods for paying on an adjustable-rate mortgage are not inflexible. You can combine both approaches to accelerating your adjustable-rate mortgage.

Example. In consideration of your current budget, you begin accelerating as shown in the second plan, paying at a rate 1 percent higher than the interest you're being charged. A few years later, you can afford to accelerate beyond that level, so you decide to increase your payment to the highest rate under the terms of your contract.

How do the numbers work out? Based on the example we've been using (five-point lifetime cap, 1 percent annual cap, $80,000 mortgage starting at 8 percent, amortized on a 30-year term), here's how you could convert at the end of the second year: At that point, the mortgage is being paid at the rate of $702.06 per month, the 10 percent rate as applied to current interest of 9 percent. The lender raises the rate to 10 percent. The plan calls for an increase to $761.86 per month. However, you decide to pay $885, so the acceleration method is converted over to the first plan.

Because the gradual increase method does not accelerate as rapidly as the fixed payment method, chances are the rate will have to be raised again in the future. But for the moment, the effect of this change is to accelerate beyond the level of the original plan.

In the event you start an acceleration plan and must later cancel it, your payments will revert to the lower required amount, based on the current balance and effective interest rate. With a 30-year term, this contingency is allowed for, giving you the most flexibility. The long-term payment requirement will be lower than it would be on (1) a 15-year amortization schedule or (2) the payment due without any acceleration during the early years.

Your flexibility will not be limited to merely changing the terms of the plan. You will also be able to revert back to the minimum required payment during the term of the loan. Your lender will calculate the amount of payment required based on the years until full amortization, modified by the actual balance due.

Example. The current interest rate on an adjustable-rate loan is 11 percent, and the loan has 18 years to go under its original term. The monthly payment the lender will require at various loan balances is as follows:

Loan Balance	Monthly Payment
$30,000	$319.52
40,000	426.02
50,000	532.53
60,000	639.03

Obviously, the greater the rate of acceleration during the earlier years, the lower the minimum balance required to continue amortizing that loan. Thus, in the event you need to suspend acceleration, your monthly payment will be lower following a period of substantial extra payments.

In considering an acceleration plan, whether your mortgage is set up with a fixed or an adjustable rate, you must recognize that the money you put into the plan cannot be easily taken back. We have mentioned the need for an emergency reserve fund in previous chapters. In the next chapter, you will see how the need for this fund can be coordinated with a reasonable plan for reducing the overall cost of your home.

7 THE EMERGENCY RESERVE FUND

A family must establish a savings of ready cash before beginning a complete plan of acceleration. Once you put money into additional equity payments, it cannot be taken back out easily.

The emergency reserve fund is created as protection in the event of an unexpected need for cash. If you lose your job, for example, you will need at least a minimum reserve fund just to meet your expenses until income starts up again.

CUTTING MONTHLY EXPENSES

If your income ceases unexpectedly, your first step should be to seek a way to reduce your monthly expenses. If you have already accelerated mortgage payments, you might be able to talk your lender into suspending payments for three to six months. Of course, that means the balance will rise, due to the continuing accumulation of interest on the unpaid balance.

Even if you have not accelerated your payments, your lender might be willing to delay receiving payments for a limited number of months. As long as you have some equity built up (from the combination of payments and increased market value), most lenders would rather work with you than end up having to foreclose on your home.

If you run into this situation, visit with your lender and explain your temporary hardship. Your position should be that you fully intend to resume payments as soon as you restore your monthly income and that you understand interest will accumulate each month. By letting the lender know there's a problem before you fall behind in scheduled payments, you are more likely to get a friendly and cooperative response.

The same step can be taken with other lenders. If you have unpaid balances on store charge accounts, revolving credit cards, and bank loans, chances are that most lenders will give you a grace period of a few months—especially if you communicate with them rather than just not making your payments.

If you have a history of prompt payments and a strong credit rating, you will certainly find that lenders will work with you in most cases. But some will not. A few will remain inflexible, demanding timely payments and threatening legal action, repossession, or foreclosure if those payments are not made. For these lenders, your emergency reserve fund will be essential. If your mortgage lender is one of the people who will not allow you to delay payments, you will certainly need your emergency reserve fund.

As to how much you should put into savings, there are various opinions. Some advisors suggest three months' income should be saved; others say six. Some families will have great difficulty accumulating a savings account equal to half a year's income; others will find it an absolute necessity. The right level for you depends on the following factors:

1. The level of monthly expenses for necessities and recurring payments.

2. Your credit history, and the way lenders would respond if asked for a grace period in making recurring payments.

3. Sources of borrowing. For example, many families today have large credit lines on various accounts. It is not unusual for a family with four or five charge cards to have $20,000 or more in lines of credit. The problem with using those credit lines, however, is that it only increases your debt. You must be able to budget for repayments later.

4. Your ability to save. Some families budget a regular amount from each paycheck and put that amount into a savings account or other investments every month, without fail. Others never seem to have anything left over. A lot depends on your income level and on whether one or both spouses work.

With all these points in mind, you must decide for yourself what is the necessary amount to have in a cash fund. If you have two sources of income, you have a greater ability to put money away—and you also have less at risk in the event that one income ceases. That second salary would certainly help to continue payments for necessities.

BUDGETING A SAVINGS PLAN

An emergency reserve fund should be set up in an account where you can get the money as quickly as possible—an account in a local bank or savings and loan or in a credit union, for example. Or you can open an account with a money market mutual fund. These no-load funds invest in short-term government and corporate notes, certificates of deposit, bankers acceptances, and other instruments. Most funds also supply you with blank checks, so that you can withdraw your savings simply by completing and cashing one.

Build a reasonable amount of money into your budget to start an emergency reserve fund, if you have not already established one. You should set the level so that you can afford to continue deposits, even when unexpected expenses arise. Many financial advisors call this paying yourself first. If you earn a total of $2,000 per month, for example, set aside $100 or $200 per month as a savings, and budget your other expenses with what's left over.

Like all forms of savings, a regular and permanent program requires discipline. There's no point in starting a savings plan if you remove the money a few months later. It should be kept for absolute emergencies. Otherwise, you defeat your own purpose.

We tend to adjust our life-style to our incomes. So when income increases, so do expenses. If you begin a regular savings program and stick with it every month, you will develop the habit of doing without the small amounts you put away. A mortgage acceleration plan is one form of forced savings, because that money cannot be taken back and used for other reasons. Once the payment is made, the money is gone.

A savings account is much different. You can get the money out whenever you want, so there's more temptation to misuse an emergency reserve fund. Your total, overall financial plan should include a division of cash into several distinct categories, and no one category should be used for any purpose other than you intend. These include

Savings (emergency reserve fund)

Monthly expenses (mortgage payments, food, utilities, home maintenance, clothing, automobile expense, insurance premiums, other)

Investments

The order of the list should also be the order of priority in your budget. The first category, savings, is a relatively small part of your budget, but it should be automatic each and every paycheck.

The second group is where most of your income will go. The necessities on which you spend money take up the majority of most paychecks. The last item, "other," is where a lot of people run into problems. Vacations and recreation, purchasing luxury items, and those miscellaneous expenses that are difficult to even identify at the end of the month can add up to a huge amount of money each year. That is the area where you can exercise the greatest amount of control. By reducing "other" expenses, you will have more left over for the third category.

Your investments may include the purchase of mutual fund shares, stocks, and a variety of other choices. They can also include mortgage acceleration.

Just as proceeding without an emergency reserve fund is not prudent, it is also a mistake to put all your investment money into any one place. This fact is a basic premise of investing, one that most advisors recognize. The need for diversification is absolute.

Just as you might split your investment fund between direct ownership of stocks, mutual funds, and savings bonds, a portion can also be put into mortgage acceleration.

DESIGNING YOUR OWN PLAN

You can eliminate payments to an emergency reserve fund once you reach the level you need (based on the risks to which you're exposed in the event your income stops or the level and frequency of unexpected expenses). You might need to increase your fund from time to time, since your financial status will change over the years. But to a large extent, this changing need will be offset by the interest your fund will be earning.

Example. A family establishes an emergency reserve fund at a balance of $6,000, equal to three months' income. In a 6 percent savings account on which interest is compounded quarterly, this fund will increase over time, even without additional payments:

Year	Balance
1	$ 6,368.18
2	6,758.96
3	7,173.71
4	7,613.91
5	8,081.13
10	10,884.11
15	14,659.32

In gradually building a fund over several years, the savings can be coordinated with mortgage acceleration. For example, if you assume that in your budget there's a total of $200 per month available for savings and investing, both an emergency reserve fund and a mortgage acceleration plan can be started at the same time.

Figure 7–1 shows how both are scheduled. During the first year, the entire $200 per month goes toward the emergency re-

YEAR	Yearly payments to: RESERVE FUND	MORTGAGE
1	$2,400	$ 0
2	1,800	600
3	1,200	1,200
4	600	1,800
5–on	0	2,400

Figure 7–1 Coordinating the reserve fund, $200 per month

serve fund, for a total of $2,400. In the second year, $50 per month is put toward accelerating the mortgage, and $150 goes into the emergency reserve fund. Each year thereafter, the emergency reserve fund deposit is reduced by $50 per month, as the acceleration level is increased. By the fifth year, the entire $200 goes toward mortgage payments. At that point, the $6,000 emergency reserve has been created.

Why not build the emergency reserve fund first and then accelerate later? That is one alternative, and it should be done that way if you are at great risk. For example, if your family depends solely on one income and you cannot afford to lose three months' income, you should build the entire fund before any other form of investing is done. However, many people will find that a gradually created fund is adequate. And the earlier you begin an acceleration plan, the greater its benefits.

For example, in the plan just described, how much interest will be saved over the term of the mortgage? Using the example of an $80,000 loan at 10 percent, amortized over a 30-year term, the required payment is $702.06 per month. Under the plan just presented, payments increase gradually over the first five years:

Year	Mortgage Payments
1	$702.06
2	752.06
3	802.06
4	852.06
5–on	902.06

On this schedule, the mortgage will be paid off in 15 years and 7 months, rather than in 30 years, and the total amount saved will be more than $90,000. The comparison of gradually increased mortgage payments and minimum payments over 30 years is shown in Figure 7–2.

THE BALANCED PLAN

The need for an emergency reserve fund and the desirability of reduced interest expense do not necessarily conflict. You do not have to select one over the other but can have both.

It requires a balanced approach. Think of it as a form of diversification. On the one hand, you create a highly liquid (available) fund of cash in a safe, low-yielding savings account; on the other hand, you apply the appropriate amount of money toward equity and reduce the cost of your home by $90,000.

Mortgage acceleration, in one respect, is a form of supplemental emergency reserve. In the event that you need to borrow money in the future, a larger amount of equity increases the amount you could borrow. Building equity quickly reduces your home's cost; however, you can also look at it as a source for borrowed money.

Compare remaining balances on your loan, both with and without acceleration (see the second appendix). In the example of a gradually accelerated loan, how do the remaining balances com-

	FULL AMORTIZATION	GRADUAL INCREASE	SAVINGS
total months	360	187	
total payments	$252,735	$ 162,016	$ 90,719
less: principal	80,000	80,000	
interest	$172,735	$ 82,016	$ 90,719

Figure 7–2 Plan comparisons

pare? At the rate of 10 percent, the 30-year and 15-year, 7-month plans come out as follows:

Year	Remaining Balance 30 Years	15 Years
5	96.6%	87.9%
10	90.9	57.2
15	81.7	6.8
20	66.4	0
25	41.3	
30	0	

If your house originally cost $100,000 and grows in value to $125,000 within several years, your total borrowing power will be greater after an accelerated repayment plan. Most lenders will allow you to take out a second mortgage or to refinance up to 80 percent of your home's current market value. Once equity is computed, you must subtract the balance of loans outstanding to find out how much you have in borrowing power: available equity, less existing loan balances.

Let us compare potential borrowings:

1. After 5 years:

	30 Years	15 Years
Current value	$125,000	$125,000
Less: 20% equity	25,000	25,000
80%	$100,000	$100,000
Less: Loan balance	77,259	70,283
Borrowing power	$ 22,741	$ 29,717

2. After 10 years:

	30 Years	15 Years
Current value	$125,000	$125,000
Less: 20% equity	25,000	25,000
80%	$100,000	$100,000
Less: Loan balance	72,750	45,785
Borrowing power	$ 27,250	$ 54,215

3. After 15 years:

	30 Years	15 Years
Current value	$125,000	$125,000
Less: 20% equity	25,000	25,000
80%	$100,000	$100,000
Less: Loan balance	65,330	5,477
Borrowing power	$ 34,670	$ 94,523

With full amortization, your equity builds so slowly that you have no substantial equity even after 15 years. Most of the equity available from borrowing in these examples comes with the assumption that the house has increased in value to $125,000.

In comparison, the accelerated mortgage builds equity rapidly over the same 15-year schedule. You would have much more safety with this plan, in the sense that your much higher equity represents higher borrowing power.

USING BUILT-UP EQUITY

The question of an emergency reserve fund comes up not only when a family first buys a house but again when the family sells and moves elsewhere.

Example. A family sells its home and receives $80,000 cash after all costs and after paying for a move. The family buys a new home for $125,000.

The following question comes up at this point: How much should be put toward a down payment? The tempting move is to put down only the minimum and invest the balance somewhere else. But this plan is not always the wisest alternative, even though it does create a substantial emergency reserve fund.

The first problem with putting the minimum down is that the large cash balance will not necessarily be used as you originally intend. You might end up spending the money rather than saving it.

The second problem is that you again face a high cost of interest by financing most of your new purchase. With a second home, you again have the power to determine and to control the ultimate cost of housing for yourself and your family.

The third problem is that even if you do invest the money and leave it intact, it's a higher level for emergencies than you probably need. You could do much better by using that cash to reduce your debts. Figure 7–3 shows three alternatives in this situation.

With the first plan, you have $55,000 left over, but interest adds up to $215,929 over the next 30 years. Compared to the last plan, calling for a 60 percent down payment, that's double the interest expense.

When you keep out a large part of your equity from a previous home's sale and put the minimum down on a new house, you are, in effect, removing a portion of that equity. But in order to do so, you must finance a higher balance. Thus, you are borrowing more money than you need to.

An argument against putting the entire balance down is that you have many years to make that fund grow in value. But you should ask yourself the following question: If I had not moved, would I have borrowed that money to invest?

The answer to that question is probably no, because most people know that it is difficult to earn more than the amount that must be paid in loan interest. Now, having moved to a new home, you have the same question, but it is phrased differently: Do you want a $100,000 mortgage or a $50,000 mortgage?

With a smaller mortgage balance, you have lower monthly payments—perhaps lower than those you were making on your previous home. These lower payments give you the flexibility to

AMOUNT PREPAID	AMOUNT SAVED	MONTHS SAVED
$ 100	$ 1,984	2.8
400	7,935	11.3
700	13,886	19.8
1,000	19,837	28.3

Figure 7–3 Buying a second home, $80,000 equity to invest. Interest is calculated as 10% mortgage, 30-year term

save and invest more money each month, perhaps even to create a new acceleration plan.

Example. A family previously had a mortgage payment of $702.06 per month. When they sold their home, they had $80,000 in equity. They bought a home for $125,000 and put 60 percent, or $75,000, down and had $5,000 in cash left over. This amount, added to the emergency reserve fund they already had, was more than enough cash. They then committed to a 30-year term on a 10 percent mortgage, with a balance of $50,000, requiring monthly payments of $438.79. However, they were accustomed to paying more than $700 per month and decided to accelerate at about the same rate. Their payments of $703.94 each month paid off the entire loan in nine years. The difference in interest was $81,938.

Your emergency reserve fund should be a higher priority than any acceleration plan. However, once you have established a reasonable level, avoid the temptation to build it beyond that point. Diversify the available money you have between acceleration and other worthwhile investments, and you will be able to reduce your housing costs with very little risk.

In the next chapter we shall explore how and why the common arguments against acceleration are often flawed. Any evaluation of alternatives must be made with all the information you need concerning true after-tax returns, risks, and the high cost of borrowing money.

8 THE FLAWED ARGUMENTS

Even with the benefits you gain by reducing the cost of your home and the repayment term for your mortgage, lenders and salespeople still insist that speeding up your payments is a poor idea. However, once you have established an adequate emergency reserve fund, acceleration will prove to be a worthwhile investment in most circumstances.

In previous chapters, many of these arguments were introduced. In this chapter, we will present a detailed examination of the arguments. We will also look at the circumstances where acceleration is not a good idea.

THE POPULAR ARGUMENT

To evaluate an argument, you must always consider the source. The strongest case against mortgage acceleration is made by lenders and by people who sell investment securities.

Lenders benefit when you borrow money or when you pay off a loan over the longest possible period. The more acceleration you achieve, the lower the lender's total income. Lenders are in the money business, meaning that they have an inventory of capital working for them in the form of loans. The longer the repayment period, the higher the use of that inventory.

Salespeople are interested in getting you to borrow money with equity as collateral, because that means more commission income for them. There is no commission paid on acceleration, so salespeople cannot be expected to objectively compare advantages between investments on which they earn money and strategies on which they receive nothing.

Here's the salesperson's dilemma: You, as a potential client, might be very interested in the opportunities of investing in the stock market, mutual funds, public syndications, or annuities. But you have a limited amount of cash. If the salesperson's commission is 8 percent, the amount of income to be earned depends on the amount invested. If you put in $2,000, the total commission is only $160. But if you invest $20,000, the commission jumps to $1,600.

With that in mind, many salespeople appeal to your sense of guilt about how and why you should borrow as much as possible and why you must put your home equity to work. The presentation includes these arguments:

1. You need the tax deduction you get from paying interest on your mortgage.

2. Acceleration is a poor idea. You're better off paying over the full term and investing your "disposable income" somewhere else.

3. As time goes on, acceleration is expensive because inflation erodes the buying power of your money. Thus, you're prepaying a fixed mortgage with dollars that are worth increasingly less.

4. You have all that equity just sitting in your home. You should take it out and put it to work.

These arguments often work because they appeal to common apprehensions that most of us have.

Income Taxes

Taxation is complicated, especially in light of recent legislation. So salespeople like to make arguments favoring higher deductions—even when the true after-tax cost of their advice is higher than an acceleration plan's outcome.

Salespeople use this argument: When you pay a mortgage at 10 percent and your tax rate is 28 percent, your after-tax mortgage costs you only 7.2 percent. That sounds very attractive—until you realize that the investment you make on the outside is also taxable at your effective rate.

Missing Investment Opportunities

A common misconception is that investment salespeople have some form of knowledge that the ordinary person does not. The aura of expertise is created partly by the titles many salespeople use, like financial planner, advisor, or consultant. It also comes from a general assumption that the financial community is highly sophisticated, and that is not necessarily true.

Anyone can call themselves a financial planner, and even those who have many years of experience often come from a singular discipline. Their background may be in life insurance, mutual fund sales, or the stock market. Chances are they don't understand real estate *or* the real cost of buying a home due to interest expenses.

Inflation Fears

The word "inflation" is a scare word. We are conditioned to fear it, even though the rate in the United States, compared to other countries, has been relatively low in most periods.

Salespeople like to point to past performance of the investments, claiming they beat inflation. This practice implies that a particular investment will always beat inflation and that it somehow protects you from the consequences of reduced buying power.

Guilt Concerning Idle Equity

The argument that it's foolish to leave your equity idle is probably the most flawed of all arguments. Equity is a valuable asset, and when you borrow it or when you do not practice acceleration, you're paying a lot of money in interest. You should ask yourself whether you would borrow money to invest if you did not own a home. Most people would not. Yet, that's exactly what you're doing when you "take out" your idle equity.

Financial planners like to use terms like *disposable income* to describe money available to invest. But when they include your home equity, it's an extremely irresponsible approach. You must make a distinction between income and assets. Income is spent, while assets should be preserved and their value built up over time. A portion of your income is converted to permanent asset value when you make payments toward the principal portion of your mortgage. If you later borrow money secured by equity, you actually convert the asset back into "disposable" income.

THE FACTS

The arguments used by salespeople to free up money (and generate a commission) are flawed, even without evaluating the reasons to accelerate your mortgage payments

Income Taxes

You never *need* a tax deduction that is derived from higher expenses. Paying less interest is always better, even when deductions are reduced as a result.

Make the comparison using any interest and tax rate you want. You will never be able to establish a true after-tax benefit from higher deductions. The net cost of reduced interest is always lower than the cost of higher interest and maximum deductions. Salespeople like to compare after-tax interest costs to before-tax investment yields, which is a faulty comparison.

Example. If you apply a 28 percent tax rate against a 10 percent mortgage, the net is 7.2 percent. How does that compare to a mutual fund that has historically yielded 9 percent? In fact, the taxable mutual fund proceeds reduce that yield to 6.48 percent:

	Mortgage	Investment
Before-tax cost/yield	10.00%	9.00%
Tax deduction/penalty	−2.80	2.52
After-tax cost/yield	7.20	6.48

Missing Investment Opportunities

Investment opportunities that are bought with borrowed funds are rarely as sound as an acceleration program. In making that argument, salespeople avoid comparing risk. With acceleration, there is virtually no risk; with just about any other type of investment, an equivalent yield will carry a substantial level of risk.

Inflation Fears

Don't be misled by the argument that your dollars will be worth less in the future. While inflated prices do reduce your buying power, the inflation argument has nothing to do with a comparison between acceleration and other investments.

Example. You will make a $1,000 investment in 10 years. If that $1,000 has a reduced buying power as the result of inflation, it will be worth less whether it's paid toward reduced mortgage interest or for the purchase of mutual fund shares.

Guilt Concerning Idle Equity

This argument is the favorite of both lenders and salespeople. You're supposed to believe that building equity is an example of poor financial management, that you're missing the chance to invest smartly, and that sophisticated people are always in debt to the maximum.

The fact is that leverage can be an expensive and risky strategy. The more you owe, the more you must repay, and the longer you will remain in debt. This argument is meant to put your equity to work for the lender or the salesperson, not for you.

COMPARING RISKS

Compare the actual risks of the advice you receive. For a lender, a mortgage is secured by your home, so the risk is minimal. If you're unable to make payments, the lender will foreclose and sell your home, getting all its money back. And for the salesperson, a commission is paid at the time the investment is made. There's no risk for a salesperson.

All of the risk is yours. Even if you believe you can earn interest that is equal to or better than the benefits of acceleration, you must be able to earn that rate every year, for many years to come, because your mortgage debt will continue for as long as 30 years. You might be able to lock in a good rate this year, but what about in five years? Or ten? There's no guarantee that the favorable yield from an investment will continue, as it does from acceleration.

To demonstrate, assume you have just committed to a 30-year mortgage for $80,000. Your first payment is coming due this month, and you have some money to invest. Your rate is 10 percent, and the mortgage term is 30 years. To match this yield, you must be able to find an investment that will yield you 10 percent, compounded monthly, and that will pay that much consistently, for the next 30 years.

The value of making even a single payment toward principal, at the first month you begin paying your mortgage, is substantial. If you pay $100 extra (making your first payment $802.06 instead of $702.06), that single accelerated payment is worth $1,984 and cuts 2.8 months off the total repayment term. A $1,000 prepayment takes 28.3 months off the term (more than four years) and yields a return of $19,837. Samples of single payments at the beginning of a mortgage term are shown in Figure 8–1.

To match these returns, you must be able to put the same amount into an investment that will yield 10 percent (compounded monthly) for the next 30 years. Not only will you be unlikely to find such an investment, but

1. It's unlikely you will find one as safe as investing in your own home.

2. There's the risk factor to consider. To match the mortgage rate you're paying, you will have to accept the possibility that the value of your outside investment could fall.

3. Money invested outside of your mortgage will probably be more available than it is when put into your home. Thus, there's

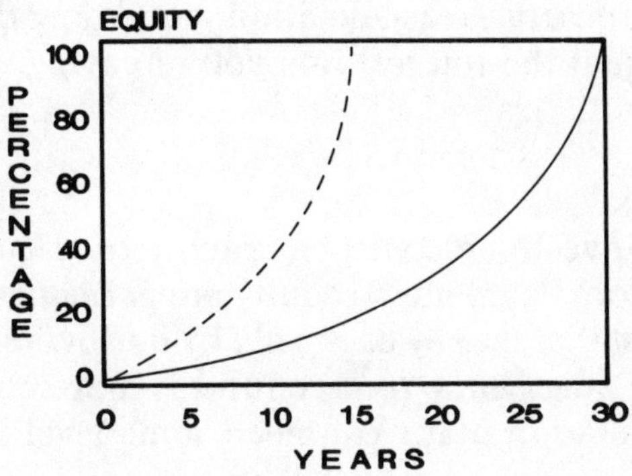

Figure 8–1 Single payment acceleration, $80,000 loan, 30-year term, 10%. —, scheduled payments; - - -, accelerated payments

a greater chance you'll spend that money within the next 30 years—your asset will be converted to disposable income.

The 10 percent comparison has been made on a before-tax basis. But unless you can get a yield equal to your mortgage in a tax-free investment, you will be taxed on your profits. So while mortgage acceleration reduces tax benefits, outside investments increase taxable income. If the yields from both are equal, the tax consequences are equal, too.

EVALUATING RISKS

Any form of investing may be risky in many respects. To make a valid comparison between acceleration and other alternatives, be sure to include all forms of risk, including the following forms.

Yield

Chances are that even if you can obtain a high yield today, you won't be able to match it for as long as your mortgage term. Very few investments can be projected that far, even with guaranteed rates. But with mortgage acceleration, you know that your yield will always equal the interest rate you're paying.

Liquidity

Most outside investments will be much more liquid than mortgage acceleration. Payments to equity are permanent in the sense that you can get that money back only by borrowing in the future. That's why an emergency reserve fund is a prerequisite to your personal acceleration plan. You need some level of liquidity.

Capital Value

You might suffer from reverses in the market. For example, if your \$20,000 investment loses 20 percent of its value, you're out \$4,000. Not only is your capital worth less, but you have a smaller base from which to earn a yield.

One argument against acceleration is that housing values may not increase as rapidly as other investments. But remember, you owe your mortgage balance to the lender and must pay it. The ultimate investment value of your home is not the issue. Rather, the true cost, including interest on your debt, should be the basis for comparison.

Diversification

There is risk in putting all your money into any one investment. That includes acceleration of your mortgage. Some portion of your total money should be put into your emergency reserve fund, a retirement plan, and other investments.

Besides evaluating relative risks, view your mortgage realistically. It's a debt. When you "take out" your equity, you're borrowing money to invest or to spend. You must either allow your debt to amortize over the full term or go further into debt by committing to a new mortgage. Many people would simply not borrow money to invest but will readily use their home equity.

Example. A homeowner has enough equity to take out a new mortgage of \$20,000. A financial advisor suggests taking that step and investing the $20,000 in a diversified portfolio. The arguments are the usual ones: Equity is being put to work, the interest is deductible, and the outside investment is better than leaving equity alone.

Example. A renter is approached by a salesperson, who suggests investing $20,000 in a diversified portfolio. But the renter has no cash to invest, so he or she goes to the bank and requests a $20,000 loan.

Both the homeowner and the renter have done the same thing: borrowed money to invest. In the first case, it's widely accepted that using equity is a prudent financial move. In the second case, the renter applies for a loan that will not be secured by real estate. Most people, even financial planners, will agree that borrowing money to invest is not a smart idea. Yet, homeowners are constantly encouraged to do just that.

Acceleration must be evaluated as one of many possible investments, because the reduction of interest expense is the same thing as earning interest. Either you reduce expenses or earn additional income. The real difference is that acceleration does not yield a commission for a salesperson, and it reduces the lender's overall income.

THE TIME FACTOR

The total period of debt is one form of risk that is often overlooked. In comparing and evaluating your choices, keep this risk in mind. With your mortgage, the time factor is a significant point. In a 30-year mortgage term, you are at risk in the sense that you might be unable to continue payments. If you lose your job, if you have health problems, if you're disabled, or if other expenses arise, you are at risk.

With acceleration, a small addition to monthly payments will cut many years off the period of risk. Besides reducing the cost of your home, acceleration will reduce the time risk. In comparison, investing outside of your mortgage increases your risk exposure by continuing the debt over the full term.

On an $80,000 mortgage at 10 percent and with a 30-year term, adding $25 per month cuts the repayment period by five years. Besides enjoying a 10 percent yield on the $25 per month investment, you cut five years from your risk exposure period.

Compare investments with both yield and time in mind, and evaluate mortgage acceleration in two ways:

Single Payments to Principal

Compare a $100 deposit at the beginning of your mortgage term to a $100 deposit in another investment. Keep in mind that

1. The yield from acceleration is constant over the entire period.
2. The only real risk is that the acceleration plan is illiquid.

A Series of Payments Added Each Month

Compare the value of adding minimal amounts to principal each month. Evaluate

1. The total reduction in the cost of your home that comes from lower interest payments
2. The reduction in the months or years required to pay off your mortgage

The financial advantages you gain by reducing your repayment period are conveniently overlooked by those who discourage acceleration. When you enter an agreement for a 30-year repayment term on your mortgage, you are committed to making timely payments every month. But by reducing that term, you build equity and future flexibility in several ways.

Budget Flexibility

The rate of acceleration can be suspended or reduced as circumstances change. A realistic plan will be set up to suit your budget now, but if you have unexpected expenses or lower income in the future, you can modify your plan.

Example. A family with two working spouses starts accelerating its 30-year mortgage at the 15-year rate. Two years later, the husband loses his job and is out of work for three months. During that period, the couple pays the smaller 30-year payment. When the husband finds a new job, they resume their accelerated payment plan.

Future Savings

Your budget adjusts itself to a changing income level. Most families aren't able to save more when their incomes rise, because their budgets rise along with higher available cash. Acceleration forces you into the savings habit. And when your loan is paid off earlier, that means more savings in the future.

Example. A family accelerates its 30-year mortgage at the 15-year rate. When the loan is fully paid off, the family continues putting the same amount away each month. However, instead of going to a lender, that money goes into savings and investments. The family pays less for its home and is able to save a significant amount of money each month after the mortgage has been paid off.

If the original loan was $80,000 and the interest rate was 10 percent, the difference in the monthly mortgage payment is about $158 per month, or payments of $859.69. After 15 years, the family continues to save this amount each month. By the time the original loan was scheduled for repayment—15 years later—the total of savings and investment will be more than $150,000, before interest is even figured. This family wins in two ways: by reducing the cost of its home by $98,000 and by building a substantial savings and investment program by the end of the 30-year term.

Future Borrowing Power

When you increase equity more rapidly, you also increase the amount available to you in the future. Many families consider home equity as a source for secured debt, and that's a valid way to look at your home.

Example. A family buys a house and, several years later, needs more space. Rather than move, the family decides to add on. The improvements are financed with the built-up equity. By refinancing its mortgage, the family pays for extra living space.

MORTGAGES AND TAX STRATEGIES

Borrowing power has always been one of the most attractive features of buying real estate. As long as market values continue to rise, additional equity is created even when a mortgage is not accelerated. In the past, this enabled people to borrow money beyond the equity they had built up just from monthly payments to principal.

Example. A family bought a house in 1972, paying $29,000. By 1980, that same house had a market value of $125,000. The original $23,200 mortgage, which had a rate of 7.5 percent, had been reduced to $21,000. Still, with a higher market value, there was much more available in equity:

Market value	$125,000
Maximum loan, 80%	$100,000
Less: Loan balance	21,000
Available to borrow	$ 79,000

So although the purchase price was only $29,000 and only $8,000 was paid toward equity, the homeowner could borrow as much as $79,000 more.

Part of the advantage in borrowing equity used to be that the interest was fully tax deductible. But the Tax Reform Act of 1986 curtailed that benefit considerably. Beginning in 1987, you have been able to deduct interest on your home mortgage only to the extent that the money you borrow does not exceed your basis in the property. If you owned your home before August 16, 1986 and had already borrowed more than your basis, then the effective limit under this rule was the amount you owed as of August 16, 1986.

Example. The homeowner who paid $29,400 in 1972 had taken out a new mortgage and, on August 16, 1986, owed a total of $51,000. For purposes of deducting interest expense, that homeowner's basis is $51,000.

If you bought your home after August 16, 1986, your basis is the adjusted purchase price, plus any permanent improvements made to your home. So if your home's market value rises to the point that you can qualify for a loan above your basis, you will be limited in what you can deduct. If you use mortgage proceeds to add to your home, your basis is increased by that amount, and all your interest is still deductible. But if you spend the money on a new car, debt consolidation, and a trip to Europe, you will not be allowed to deduct a portion of the interest.

Example. You bought a home for $100,000 two years ago and now want to borrow $20,000 through a second mortgage. Interest on the portion of the $20,000 above your basis will not be deductible on your tax return.

This new restriction appears punitive at first glance. But, in fact, it is an advantage, and it presents an opportunity. The advantage comes from the fact that homeowners will be forced to maintain a minimum amount of home equity. Because deductions are cherished so highly, fewer people will borrow above their basis. The new rule also curtails the past abuses by salespeople, who encouraged homeowners to borrow the maximum to invest.

The opportunity in the new law is that acceleration is even more beneficial now than under the older system. The more you accelerate payments today, the greater the amount of equity above your original basis. There is no longer a tax advantage in borrowing against equity from higher market value. If you want to deduct your interest expense, it must be on mortgage balances below your basis.

Example. You purchased your home for $100,000 five years ago. With a $20,000 downpayment, your $80,000 mortgage amortizes over a 30-year term, at 10 percent interest. After five years, you have built up only $2,741 in equity above your basis. That, added to your down payment, equals a maximum equity of $22,741. If you borrow any more than that amount, part of your interest will not be deductible.

If that same loan had been accelerated at the 15-year rate, you would have built up $14,947 in equity. With the $20,000 down payment, you could borrow up to $34,947 without losing any interest deductions. Equity builds more rapidly in the shorter term, as shown in Figure 8–2.

You will still benefit from increased market value, whether or not you accelerate your mortgage. But given that you can deduct interest only to the extent of your original basis (plus improvements), the higher market value of your home helps you only if

1. You increase your mortgage balance for home improvements, which increase your allowed basis.
2. You sell your home, meaning more cash to you.
3. You are willing to borrow money without the subsidy of itemized deductions.

How important are itemized deductions to you? On an $80,000 mortgage at 10 percent, amortized over a 30-year term, the first five years of the loan term involve a total of $39,353 in interest

	20% DOWN	40% DOWN	60% DOWN
purchase price	$125,000	$125,000	$125,000
down payment	25,000	50,000	75,000
finance balance	$100,000	$ 75,000	$ 50,000
interest	$215,929	$161,945	$107,964
reserve fund	$ 55,000	$ 30,000	$ 5,000

Figure 8–2 Future borrowing power. $80,000 equity to invest. Interest calculations assume a 10 percent mortgage, 30-year term

payments. If your tax rate is 28 percent, the value of itemized deductions is $11,019 in reduced tax bills over those five years. So if you mortgage your home $80,000 above your basis, you will lose this benefit.

WHEN NOT TO ACCELERATE

A tax incentive should never be a motive to avoid a loan you must have or to forego acceleration when it will reduce your home's cost. It's just one of the many factors to include in your comparison.

Even with the glaring flaws of the popular arguments against acceleration, there are times when you should not begin a program, or when you should reduce or stop accelerated payments.

There are only three circumstances when acceleration is a poor idea. They are as follows:

When You Can't Afford It. If your budget is so restricting that you can barely afford the monthly payment you must make, acceleration will have to wait. If, in the future, you achieve budget relief from eliminating some expenses or from a higher monthly income, you should then consider starting an acceleration plan.

Before You Set up a Reserve. If your budget does not allow for acceleration today, chances are you also cannot afford to establish an emergency reserve fund. The reserve should always be a higher priority than acceleration, even when the long-term benefits are greater. You must take care of the risks you face today; otherwise, you will regret putting money into equity later on, when you need that money back.

When Other Rates Are Better. Interest rates change over time. If you have been paying on a mortgage for many years and have a low fixed rate, chances are you will be able to beat the investment value of acceleration.

Example. A family bought its home in the early 1970s and had a fixed-rate 30-year mortgage for 6 percent. In the late 1970s and early 1980s, money market rates were as high as 15 percent. In this case, acceleration made no sense, because a much higher rate could be earned elsewhere.

Of course, this comparison must also include two additional elements: risk and availability of cash. Putting cash into a money market mutual fund does contain greater risks than accelerating a mortgage, but the fund is still a fairly low-risk investment. The problem remains, however, that the money put into the fund is very liquid. If the family takes it out and spends it, then the investment comparison is meaningless. The risk and availability problems must be judged in light of the difference between the mortgage rate and the outside yield.

When interest rates in an acceptably low-risk investment fall below the mortgage rate, it then makes more sense to begin or resume an acceleration plan.

Your acceleration strategies and your comparison to other investments will vary depending on the terms of your mortgage. In the next chapter we shall explain how to pick the best mortgage terms for your own budget and repayment plan.

9 PICKING THE RIGHT MORTGAGE

One of the most frustrating tasks a home buyer must undertake can be comparing mortgage terms. At the same time you are trying to negotiate the terms of purchase, arrange for a move, and work your way through the escrow requirements, you must also become an expert on an array of mortgage terms and conditions.

To make an informed decision, you must take into consideration not only the different repayment schedules and interest rates but the total cost of one loan over another.

Due to the problem of qualifying for a lender's standards, a large number of home buyers are forced to commit to the least desirable form of mortgage. In this situation, the total cost of buying a house is raised significantly, due to the higher interest.

HOW TO MAKE THE COMPARISON

Deciding which loan is best for you means having to compare several features.

Payments for Which You Are Qualified

Example. A lender will approve a loan only when the monthly payment is no more than one-fourth of your total monthly income. If you earn $2,675 per month, the maximum payment must be no more than $668.75.

To purchase a $100,000 house with a 20 percent down payment, the financed balance is $80,000. Paid over 30 years at a fixed rate of 10 percent, the monthly payment is $702.06. You will not qualify for a 30-year loan.

However, the same lender offers an adjustable-rate mortgage that begins at 7 percent. Payments will begin at $587.02 per month (30-year term). You will qualify for this loan.

Fees Charged by the Lender

Lenders add points in varying amounts at the origination point of a loan. A point is equal to 1 percent of the loan balance. So if your lender charges two points on an $80,000 loan, you will have to pay $1,600 in points at the time your loan is approved.

Some lenders advertise attractive terms to bring in borrowers. They offer loans with no points and no appraisal fees, for example. But, chances are, you will also pay a slightly higher interest rate with that lender, meaning that over the term of repayment, the attractive terms actually cost you more.

Loan Terms

If you agree to repay your mortgage with an adjustable rate, be sure to consider the terms of each loan you compare. The initial interest rate will be increased periodically. What is the maximum interest rate increase per year, and what is the maximum for the entire term of the loan?

To make a valid comparison, you must assume that the lender will raise your rate to the maximum allowed under the contract. One lender may offer a loan beginning at 7 percent, with a maximum 1 percent annual increase and a maximum rate of 14 percent. In eight years, you could be paying the maximum. Another lender offers a similar loan that starts at 8 percent but has a four-point maximum. So you could reach the maximum in five years, but it's two percentage points lower than the other loan.

Also check prepayment rules, whether your loan is fixed or adjustable. You want to be certain that any acceleration plan you put into action will not result in a prepayment penalty.

Total Cost

What will a loan cost you over the entire repayment term? Make this comparison assuming that no acceleration occurs, so that it will be accurate.

Example. A fixed-rate loan at 10 percent should be compared to an adjustable-rate loan starting at 8 percent and rising as high as 13 percent. The lender may raise by 1 percent per year. To compare the two loans, add the points to the total of payments.

One lender charges two points for the 10 percent fixed-rate loan and no points for the adjustable-rate loan starting at 8 percent. Both loans are scheduled for a 30-year amortization. The outcome for an $80,000 loan is as follows:

	Fixed	Adjustable
Total loan payments	$252,735	$276,400
Points	1,600	0
Total cost	$254,335	$276,400

Many borrowers are attracted to the lower initial costs of the adjustable-rate loan as well as to the lower monthly payment. However, that payment rises as the rate goes up, and as it turns out, the 10 percent fixed loan will be less expensive over the full term.

Flexibility

Perhaps the most important feature to shop for is the flexibility in repayment terms. It is a mistake to shop only for low rates or minimum points in your loan. Because your financial situation will probably change drastically over the next 30 years, you will want to have the right to modify your repayment schedule. Be sure that the lender allows acceleration without penalty and that you have the right to determine whether or not to pay more than the minimum amount required.

Also be sure that *you* control the acceleration program. It might be a mistake to commit yourself to a rapid repayment schedule today. You're better off committing to a long term and then paying off the loan more rapidly.

CREATIVE FINANCING PLANS

Lenders have come up with many creative ways to allow home buyers to qualify for loans. Most of the creative financing alternatives are gimmicks designed to attract business at a very high cost. A few make buying a home convenient and affordable.

If you have trouble qualifying for a loan, the best strategy is to agree to the best terms you can get from a lender—preferably with a fixed rate and with the flexibility to increase payments without penalty. Then it's up to you to cut the cost of interest by devising and controlling your own acceleration plan.

Some of the more common forms of creative financing include the following ones.

Interest-Only Mortgages

One popular alternative to full amortization is the interest-only loan, also called the balloon mortgage. You make payments each month for the interest on your loan, and the entire balance becomes due in one final payment at the end of the mortgage term.

Example. You sign an interest-only loan for $80,000 and a 15-year term. The rate is 10 percent. You are required to pay $666.67 per month, or 10 percent interest on the full balance, for 179 months and to then make one final payment of $80,000.

The interest-only loan is designed for people who cannot otherwise qualify for a loan. But during the entire repayment term, none of the payments go toward principal.

To judge the total cost of an interest-only loan, compare it to a fully amortized loan for the same repayment term. Over 30 years, for example, the interest-only alternative costs $319,335, or $66,600 more than a fully amortized loan. And over 15 years, the loan costs $199,334, or $44,590 more than payments with principal. See Figure 9–1.

The interest-only loan might be necessary just to qualify for a loan. But if you want to reduce the cost of your home, plan to accelerate payments above the minimum required amount. This form of loan depends on increased market demand as the only form of equity building.

Buying a home is a smart investment because it enables you to build equity. But when you pay only the interest on your balance, you are still paying rent—not on an apartment, but on the money you owe to the lender. Without acceleration, this method makes your home very expensive.

I: 30–year term:	
Interest: 359 payments of $666.67	$239,335
Principal: 1 payment of $80,000	80,000
Total	$319,335
Less: 30–year amortization	252,735
Difference	$ 66,600

II: 15–year term:	
Interest: 179 payments of $666.67	$119,334
Principal: 1 payment of $80,000	80,000
Total	$199,334
Less: 15–year amortization	154,744
Difference	$ 44,590

Figure 9–1 Interest-only loans, $80,000 loan, 10%

Renegotiable-Rate Mortgages

Another way that lenders modify the terms of loans is by allowing you to make long-term repayments at a specified, fixed interest rate. But in three to five years, that rate is renegotiated. This method is also called a rollover mortgage.

In many instances, the loan is actually due in full at the end of the short period. For example, the terms specify a 10 percent loan for $80,000, to be repaid on a 30-year amortization schedule. Payments will be $702.06 per month. But the loan will be due in five years. By that point, you will have repaid only $2,741 and will owe the lender $77,259. The lender may not renegotiate the effective rate for that balance, based on the prevailing market rates at that time.

Buy-Down Mortgages

The buy-down mortgage is designed for borrowers who cannot qualify for the usual loan at current rates. A mortgage is entered at a rate well below the market, with the understanding that after a few years a higher rate will go into effect.

This mortgage often is used when you buy a home from a developer. The lender approves the loan, and the developer pays the lender the difference in interest income for the number of years the lower rate is in effect. To offset this payment, the developer charges a correspondingly higher price for the home.

Example. A developer offers a home for $100,000. At the prevailing 10 percent fixed rate, you do not qualify for financing. But under the terms of a buy-down mortgage, you are granted a 7 percent rate for three years, and that will revert to 11 percent starting with the fourth year. In this case, the lender will receive $532.25 per month for the first 36 months (as compared to $702.06 at the full 10 percent rate). That's $6,113 less income to the lender. The developer pays the lender $6,000 and then increases the home's price to $106,000.

Graduating Payment Mortgages

Under the terms of a lender-designed graduating payment plan, you start out making payments *below* the minimum required to amortize your loan and then increase payments at intervals (often three to five years).

Example. Under the lender's rules, you do not qualify for the required $702.06 monthly payments required to amortize your $80,000, 10 percent loan over 30 years. Based on your current income, you can only afford $550. So the lender proposes a graduated payment plan. You will pay $550 per month for the first three years and then increase your payments by $100 per month at three-year intervals, over a 12-year period:

Years	Payment
1–3	$550.00
4–6	650.00
7–9	750.00
10–12	850.00
13–on	950.00

With this plan, you will end up paying much more interest than with full amortization, because the loan balance will rise for the first six years. This negative amortization results because your monthly payments are less than the amount required to cover interest. The first month's payment will be broken down as follows:

Interest	$ 666.67
Principal	(116.67)
New balance	81,116.67

The interest will rise each month, because the loan's balance will be progressively higher. At the end of the second year, total payments ($550 per month for the first year and $650 for the second year) add up to $14,400; the loan's balance will be $81,828.91.

This method is an expensive way to buy a home. Not only is nothing going toward principal for the first two years, but the amount of debt increases each month. If you find yourself in a situation where the mortgage balance is rising each month, the solution is to increase payments above the minimum required to reduce the loan.

In the case presented above, paying $702.06 per month would reduce the loan on a 30-year schedule. The total additional payment required for the two-year period would be $2,449.44. The savings would equal $2,764.98:

	Scheduled Plan	Amortization Plan
Total payments	$14,400.00	$16,849.44
Difference		2,449.44
Loan balance	81,828.91	79,063.93
Difference	2,764.98	

DESIGNING YOUR OWN GRADUATING PLAN

The creative approach to mortgages may qualify you for the lender's approval terms, but it will invariably mean a much higher cost for your home. It will also mean a higher monthly payment for a greater number of months.

Under those conditions, you simply pay more money over the repayment term. The argument that the higher interest is tax deductible makes no sense, because even after taxes, you are still paying *more* than you would pay with a faster amortization.

If your goal is to reduce the cost of your home, you can design a graduating repayment schedule on your own, even when you have a very expensive mortgage. We assume here that, under the conditions of your mortgage, you are allowed to accelerate.

Example. You have an interest-only loan scheduled over 30 years. You are required to pay 10 percent interest each month on the mortgage balance of $80,000. The total balance will be due at the end of 30 years, for a total cost of $319,335.

As the first alternative, you could increase your monthly payment of $666.67 to $702.06, so that the loan will be fully amortized over the 30-year period. This method saves $66,600 in interest and also pays off the mortgage.

Additional alternatives include one of many forms of graduating payments, to reduce both the overall cost of your home and the number of years required to full repayment.

Starting with a standard 30-year mortgage at 10 percent, with a balance of $80,000, we will compare three graduating payment ideas.

The $25 Plan

Details. Increase monthly payments by $25 per month at the beginning of each year. You're required to make monthly payments of $702.06 under the mortgage term, so the first year's payments will be increased to $727.06 per month. Under this plan, the mortgage will be paid off in 15 years and 1 month (181 months), and monthly payments during the last full year will be $1,077.06:

Total of payments	$163,470
Principal	80,000
Interest	83,470

This plan is well suited for the family that expects gradual increases in monthly income over time. The mortgage is accelerated in one-half the scheduled time, but chances are that the yearly increases in mortgage payments will represent a decreasing percentage of total income each year.

The $50 Plan

Details. Start payments during the first year at the required $702.06. In the second year, increase payments by $50, and add $50 to the payment at the beginning of each year that follows. Continue this practice until the fifth year, when payments will be $902.06 per month. Continue paying $902.06 per month for the remainder of the term. Under this plan, the mortgage will be paid off in 15 years and 7 months:

Total of payments	$162,016
Principal	80,000
Interest	82,016

This plan takes six months longer than the $25 plan but costs less. To make it work, you must be able to afford a more rapid increase in monthly payments and then to maintain a repayment rate that is $200 more than the required level. If your income is expected to rise at a yearly rate of 8 percent or more over the next five years, the mortgage payment will represent a decline in total percentage of income.

The Double Principal Plan

Details. Double the amount of principal payment each month.

Example. During the first month, your required payment of $702.06 is broken down as $666.67 in interest and $35.39 in principal. The principal payment is doubled to $70.78, making the total payment $737.45. The payment level rises each month throughout the repayment term, which is 15 years and 1 month. By the last year, the payment level averages $1,300:

Total of payments	$166,891
Principal	80,000
Interest	86,891

For this plan to work, you must be able to afford the ever-growing monthly payment. During the first full year, the difference in monthly payments is $466, but by the 15th year, the difference grows to $7,487. This plan may prove less practical than the $25 and $50 plans.

A graduating plan that you design on your own is more desirable than entering a contract that is fixed by the lender. By controlling the plan yourself, you will be able to increase or decrease the rate of repayment as you desire.

The three plans above, when compared to the rate of full amortization, are not only less expensive but can be suited to fit your family's budget. Figure 9–2 shows the remaining balances at the end of five-year intervals for each plan, compared to full amortization.

THE BIWEEKLY MORTGAGE

Some lenders will allow you to pay your mortgage at one-half the monthly rate but with payments made every other week. This method is a convenient alternative to monthly payments for many people. About one-half of all the employees in the United States are paid biweekly and would prefer budgeting a mortgage payment out of each paycheck to the more traditional monthly payment.

Example. You are paid every other Friday. With a traditional monthly payment, you must budget for a large monthly payment on the first of every month. However, with a biweekly mortgage, the same amount is paid to the lender out of every check you get.

Because there are 52 weeks in the year, paying biweekly means making 26 payments per year. That's equal to one additional monthly payment per year:

Monthly payment of \$702.06 =	\$8,424.72 per year
Biweekly payment of \$351.03 =	\$9,126.78 per year
Difference =	\$702.06

An \$80,000, 10 percent loan costs \$702.06 per month; breaking it up into biweekly payments of \$351.03 will pay off the loan in 20 years, 10 months and will save \$62,728 in interest, compared to monthly payments over 30 years.

The biweekly plan will not work well if you are paid twice per month. The due dates for mortgage payments will not correspond to the dates you are paid, which will be a hardship.

		ACCELERATION METHOD		
year	30-year term	add $25 per year	add $50 per year	double principal
5	96.6%	89.8%	87.9%	91.0%
10	90.9	60.9	57.2	66.7
15	81.7	1.3	6.8	1.3
20	66.4	0	0	0
25	41.3			
30	0			

Figure 9–2 Remaining balances, graduating plans. $80,000 loan, 10%, 30-year term

Example.

Mortgage Due Date	Payday
Jan 14	Jan. 15
Jan. 28	Jan. 31
Feb. 11	Feb. 15
Feb. 25	Feb. 28
Mar. 11	Mar. 15
Mar. 25	Mar. 31

Another problem is that many lenders will not willingly accommodate a biweekly plan. If your lender is accustomed to monthly billings and payments on mortgages, a biweekly plan means the lender's computerized system will have to be changed. The computation of interest, the posting of payments, and the issuing of biweekly bills will have to be done on a completely different basis than for monthly loans.

As long as your lender will go along with a biweekly plan, this form of acceleration is easily budgeted and will save money while cutting the repayment term. But if your lender is unwilling to change its system to help you accelerate your mortgage, you will have to pick another method of repayment.

Example. You will save approximately the same amount in interest and pay off your mortgage in 20 years by adding $70 per month to your payment—the same result as with making payments on a biweekly basis.

The problems of arranging a biweekly payment directly with a lender can be overcome by signing up with Billie Mac, a program that acts as go-between for you and your lender. Billie Mac is an acronym for the Bi-weekly Mortgage Acceptance Corporation. This organization, located in Manchester, New Hampshire, charges a one-time fee to participate, and offers electronic fund transfer to make your mortgage payments for you. Funds are transferred every other week in an amount equal to one-half your monthly mortgage payment. Since there are 52 weeks per year, that means 26 transfers are made, or a total of 13 payments per year. And the extra payment built up over the 12 months is applied toward principal on your mortgage.

This program is ideal for people who are paid biweekly, since it enables them to budget an equal amount each paycheck for mortgage payments. The alternative—planning for one full payment on the first of each month—is an inconvenience. Not only is that a relatively large portion of one paycheck; it also fails to coordinate the date you are paid with the date the mortgage is due.

In theory, you could design your own biweekly program, in which you put one-half of your monthly payment into a savings account, and then pay the lender each month. But the problem is that you are likely to use that extra money for other expenses. The program offered by Billie Mac is both convenient and automatic. For many people, that is worth the one-time fee.

The Billie Mac program is called TEAM (The Equity Acceleration Method), and works equally well for fixed and variable-rate loans. People who are paid biweekly who must make a monthly mortgage payment face the budgeting dilemma whenever the payment dates are not coordinated.

In addition to arranging programs for people who are paid biweekly, Billie Mac also can arrange accelerated plans for those paid twice per month. In the usual plan, one-half of the required monthly payment is transferred automatically from your checking account to Billie Mac. They make your monthly payment for you and end up with one extra payment at the end of the year.

An interesting feature of this program is the effect of impounds or escrow payments included with your loan. For example, if your lender collects money for homeowners insurance or property taxes (in addition to principal and interest), using the Billie Mac program accelerates your mortgage still more rapidly and saves more money in interest. Because an additional payment is taken over the course of 12 months, the amount applied to impounds adds to the reduction of principal. So when your property taxes or insurance costs rise, the amount transferred rises too. And the additional transfer increases the amount of money applied to principal reduction.

Billie Mac can be contacted at The Gateway Building, 2nd Floor, 50 Phillippe Cote Street, Manchester, NH 03101 (phone: 800-234-0338 or 603-624-0024).

The specific terms under which you agree to repay your mortgage debt will determine the total cost of borrowing money, to an extent. The lower the interest rate, the less your monthly payment will be, and the lower the total cost. But going beyond the *required* repayment schedule, you can save much more. As long as you have the flexibility under your mortgage terms to accelerate the rate of repayment, the ultimate cost of borrowing is determined by the acceleration plan you use.

At the time you seek financing, a major hurdle will be qualifying for a loan, based on your monthly income and the lender's standards. This problem has led many home buyers to accept mortgage terms calling for very high interest costs. However, once your loan has been approved, the profit you make on investing in your home is decided by increased market value, coupled with your acceleration strategy. Regardless of how much your home's value grows due to changing market demand, the overall cost due to interest can be controlled and predetermined. You can identify in advance how much savings you can create by accelerating with one plan or another.

Yet another way to cut interest costs is through refinancing your mortgage debt. At times when interest rates are lower than when your mortgage was signed, you may be able to lock in a lower overall rate. The cost of transferring a loan can be more than offset by the amount you save. This strategy is the subject of the next chapter.

10 WHEN TO REFINANCE

Refinancing a debt is one form of acceleration that is practiced widely. Whenever current interest rates are lower than the rate you're paying on your existing loan, you could profit by replacing one loan with another.

The interest rate, monthly payment, and time remaining on your loan are the key points to evaluate. Paying a lower interest rate can help you to achieve three benefits:

Reduce your monthly payment without changing the total interest cost

Pay off the loan in fewer years without changing the monthly payment

Pay off your loan for the same payment and in the same number of years but put more cash in your pocket today

REFINANCING FOR BUDGET RELIEF

The first refinancing strategy does not achieve acceleration of your mortgage, nor does it lower the total interest expense. It only reduces the monthly payment.

This approach will also add years until full repayment of your mortgage and is intended for families that can benefit most from reducing their monthly expenses.

Example. One family is unable to save or invest any money and has mounting personal debts. Even with both spouses working, the cost of the mortgage is so high that they always seem to run out of money before they pay their monthly bills. However, interest rates have come down, and they can rewrite their mortgage to reduce monthly payments. That will free up money to meet their obligations and to set up an emergency reserve fund. Ultimately, they hope to also begin a long-term investment plan.

In this case, acceleration should not be a priority, because of the more immediate concerns—getting out of debt and putting some money aside for emergencies and investment.

Example. An $80,000 mortgage with a 13 percent rate and a 30-year term costs $884.96 per month. After 15 years, the outstanding balance is approximately $70,000. Refinancing can provide relief to the budget without increasing interest costs. A 20-year loan is available at 9¾ percent. That means monthly payments of $663.97, or $220.99 *less* each month. The loan will take an additional five years to repay, but the overall cost is identical to the cost with a 30-year term and a 13 percent rate:

	Total Paid
15 years at $884.96	$159,293
20 years at $663.97	$159,353

In this case, the family reduces its monthly budget by more than $200 per month for the cost of the mortgage and in exchange adds five years to its repayment term. The total cost is the same, but the debt is spread out over a longer term—an acceptable plan if budget relief is of primary importance today.

In this situation, the family may still be able to profit from acceleration *and* achieve budget relief. If, instead of paying $663.97 per month, they increase payments to $741.56, the loan will be repaid by the original term, 15 years in the future. The monthly reduction in the budget will be $143, and this will reduce overall interest expenses by $25,800.

The choice comes down to determining how much budget

relief you need today and how desirable it is to repay the entire mortgage by the original term. You can reduce your budget by $143 per month and make the original repayment date, or you can extend that date five years and reduce the budget by $220 per month.

Select the best strategy for refinancing at a lower rate with budget relief in mind, based on three points:

The amount of monthly reduction in payments

The interest savings you can achieve even with moderate acceleration

The final repayment date

REDUCING THE LOAN TERM

The second benefit of refinancing is to repay the total debt in fewer years, without substantially changing the monthly payment on the loan. This method will also reduce interest costs.

Example. Your $80,000 loan with a 30-year term and 13 percent interest involves payments of approximately $885 per month. After 15 years, the loan balance is $70,000, and the balance can be refinanced at a lower rate. By continuing to pay the same amount each month, you will reduce the years until full repayment and will save money in interest.

This example is a case of acceleration without any increased monthly cost. Even if the loan rate is reduced by only 1 percent, you will eliminate two years and a total of $20,754 of interest expense—while paying the same amount each month that you were paying before. Comparisons at various interest rates are shown in Figure 10–1.

This strategy can be applied not only through refinancing but with an adjustable-rate mortgage as well. When you are paying at the ceiling rate of 13 percent, for example, you are required to pay $885 per month. By continuing to pay that rate, even when

interest rate	monthly payment	years to repay	interest savings
13%	$885	15	
12	888	13	$20,754
11	877	12	32,934
10	876	11	43,608
9	887	10	52,884
8	911	9	60,870

Figure 10–1 Time acceleration. Original loan: 30-year term; $80,000 at 13%; balance due after 15 years, $70,000

the effective rate is lower, you will accelerate your loan balance. With this strategy, you achieve the added advantage of lower monthly payments and interest costs when the effective rate does rise.

To compute the amount you will save by reducing the interest rate and keeping the payment at the same level, refer to an interest amortization table. Find the payment being made at the original rate; then calculate the years to repayment, using the same amount but with the new rate.

Example. The 13 percent table shows a 30-year term payment of $884.96 for an $80,000 loan. If your loan balance has been reduced to $70,000 and you can refinance at the rate of 11 percent, take these steps:

1. Turn to the 11 percent table.
2. Locate the line for $70,000.
3. Find the column that contains an amount closest to $885 per month.

You will find that under the 12-year column the monthly payment is listed as $877.49. If you pay that amount each month, the loan will be fully paid in 12 years.

The process is slightly different if you use a factor table rather than monthly amount. In this type of table, the factor is the amount per dollar that is required to amortize a loan. Follow these steps:

1. Refer to the 13 percent column to identify the factor in effect at your old loan rate.

2. Find the 30-year line. The factor on this line is .0110620 and is the factor that applies to your original loan:

$$.0110620 \times \$80{,}000 = \$884.96$$

3. Divide the monthly payment ($884.96) by your current loan balance to find the factor that will apply on the amount you now owe:

$$\frac{\$884.96}{\$70{,}000} = .0126422$$

4. Refer to the 11 percent column to identify the repayment term under your refinanced rate.

5. Look for the factor closest to the factor you computed, .0126422. On the line for 12 years, the factor is .0125356. The monthly payment to eliminate your debt in 12 years is

$$.0125356 \times \$70{,}000 = \$877.49$$

When the amortization table gives you amounts, you can find the equivalent payment by checking columns. With a factor table, it's necessary to recompute the factor that applies to the current balance. That new factor is then compared to factors at the refinanced interest rate.

TAKING CASH FROM REFINANCING

A third strategy you can use in refinancing your debt is to come away with some cash in hand. At the same time, your original loan will be repaid in the same number of years.

This benefit is derived from the lower interest rate. It involves increasing the mortgage balance to free up cash but calculating a monthly payment that is approximately the same level as the payment being made at the old rate. This process will not only put cash in your hands; it will also reduce the total interest expense over the remainder of the term—acceleration that also yields cash but keeps the original payoff date intact.

Example. You are paying $884.96 per month on an original mortgage of $80,000 at 13 percent. After 15 years, you still owe $70,000, and you can refinance at 11 percent. To keep the payment at the same level and to still repay the loan in 15 years, how much cash can you obtain by refinancing?

If you are using a table with amounts, follow these steps:

1. Locate the section for 11 percent, the refinanced interest rate.
2. Find the line for $70,000, your current loan balance.
3. Check the 15-year column to find the required monthly payment. It shows $795.62.
4. Subtract $795.62 from the payment you have been making on your 13 percent loan, $884.96. The answer is $89.34.
5. Move up the 15-year column to find the payment closest to $89.34. On the line for $7,000, the payment is $79.57.
6. Subtract $79.57 from the previous balance of $89.34, leaving $9.77. Move up the 15-year column again. The required payment on the line for $800 is $9.10 per month.

When these amounts are all added together, you have calculated how much you can borrow without increasing your monthly payment:

	Borrowed	Payment
	$70,000	$795.62
	7,000	79.57
	800	9.10
Total	$77,800	$884.29

At the time you refinance, you can obtain $7,800 ($77,800 less the current balance of $70,000) and keep your monthly payment and loan term the same. In addition, the reduced interest rate lowers your total interest expense:

Total interest, 13%, 30 years, $80,000	$238,586
Less: Interest paid after 15 years	149,293
Interest, next 15 years	$ 89,293
Refinanced loan, 11%, 15 year-term, $77,800	81,372
Amount saved	$ 7,921

If you are using a factor table, such as the one shown in the Appendix 1, the calculation is simplified. Follow these steps:

1. Refer to the 11 percent column, the refinance rate.
2. Find the 15-year line. The factor for the refinanced rate is .0113660.
3. Divide your current monthly payment by the 11 percent factor to calculate the maximum you can borrow:

$$\frac{\$884.96}{.0113660} = \$77,860.29$$

To achieve the same repayment date and to keep your payment at about the same level, the maximum you can refinance is $7,860.29 higher than your current balance.

CONTROLLING COSTS AND TERMS

If you consider refinancing a method for reducing the number of years until repayment, then the loan should be repaid at the same level as your current required payment. However, if your purpose in refinancing is to reduce the monthly expense but leave the number of years intact, the required payment is easily calculated.

The important point about refinancing is to maintain control over the terms and interest expense. You have the opportunity of taking three different approaches to refinancing:

Leaving your payment level intact, so that the loan will be paid off sooner and for less interest expense

Decreasing the monthly payment so that the loan will be paid off by the original term but for less total interest

Extending the repayment term, drastically reducing your monthly payment but not increasing the total interest expense over that period of time

The best method depends on your budget and the desirability of acceleration. As with any other strategy, the cost of your loan should always be compared as an investment. What is the yield and the risk in comparison to other choices available to you? How practical is it to accelerate, given your current financial situation and keeping in mind that this is an illiquid form of investment? If you have not set up an emergency reserve fund, opt for lower payments, put the difference into savings, and then accelerate later. But if you have an adequate reserve fund, you can afford to leave your payments intact, or even to increase them to achieve more savings and a faster repayment term.

Refinancing at lower rates is invariably profitable. However, it might be necessary to refinance at a higher rate, meaning greater interest expenses and monthly payments. In this case, mortgage acceleration can be used to offset the higher expense, but before replacing a loan with another at a higher rate, compare monthly costs and *total* interest expense.

Example. A homeowner had an original loan of $80,000 with a 30-year term and 10 percent interest. Monthly payments were $702.06. Twenty years later, the balance had fallen to approximately $53,000. The owner wanted to add a new bedroom, at a cost of approximately $20,000. The lender offered a second mortgage of $20,000 with a 15-year term and a 12 percent rate, which would require monthly payments of $240.04. This mortgage, added to the first mortgage, would raise monthly payments to $942.10.

Another lender offered to refinance the first mortgage, plus the new loan of $20,000—$73,000 total—at a rate of 11 percent and with a 30-year term. The monthly payment for the new loan would be $695.20 per month.

The refinanced loan solves one problem: The monthly payment drops a few dollars rather than increasing, but on the original loan, there are only 10 years remaining. With the refinanced loan, the homeowner is paying a higher rate, and the 30-year term starts all over again.

The extended term and higher rate of the proposed refinance at 12 percent adds 20 years to a loan that originally would be paid off in 10 years. But that's not the only problem. Compare total interest costs:

	Interest
Second mortgage:	
Original loan, 10%, 30 years, 10 years to go	$ 31,247
Plus: New loan, 12%, 15 years	23,207
Total interest	$ 54,454
Refinance:	
30-year loan, 12%, $73,000 balance	$177,272
Difference	$122,818

In this comparison, you can see that in order to borrow $20,000, refinancing means adding an extra 20 years onto the repayment term, at a cost of $122,018 above the first plan of taking out a second mortgage.

For the difference in the monthly payment, it makes sense to leave the original loan intact and finance the room addition at a separate, higher rate. That will mean higher monthly payments, but the long-term cost of refinancing is prohibitive. Some alternatives to committing to a higher monthly payment for a second mortgage are as follows:

1. Find a lender that will finance the second mortgage over 30 years. At 12 percent, the payment would be $205.73, or $34.31 lower per month (however, this method would also increase total interest by more than $12,000 and would still require 30 years to repay).

2. Reduce the additional monthly payment by borrowing less and using savings to fund a portion of the room addition. For example, borrow $15,000 rather than $20,000, which would require a 15-year repayment of $180.03, a savings of $60 per month.

3. Shop for cheaper mortgage rates or hold off on the improvement until (1) rates are lower or (2) you have more cash available.

CALCULATING REFINANCE COSTS

The comparison between rates alone is not the entire refinancing story. You will also be required to pay certain costs assessed by the lender at the time your loan is replaced. The costs will include

1. Prepayment penalties. Penalties are charged by the lender for paying off a previous loan before the scheduled due date. This fee will be charged when you go to a new lender and pay off a previous loan with new loan proceeds. Some lenders will also assess a prepayment penalty even if you replace your loan with the same institution. However, in some states, lenders cannot always charge a penalty when they replace loans for their own customers.

2. Points, based on the amount of the new loan. Points will be assessed even when no new money is actually borrowed. For example, your lender charges three points. Your current loan balance is $60,000, and you're refinancing at a lower rate. You will be charged $1,800 in points for the new loan, even though the amount of debt is not changed.

3. Other fees. The lender will probably charge for appraisal, title search, recording fees, transfer fees and tax, notary fees, credit investigation, loan processing, and a variety of other expenses. You might also be assessed an escrow fee.

The total of all your refinance costs will vary greatly depending on the points and prepayment penalty level. And the manner in which these costs are handled will affect your new loan balance and the required monthly payment.

Example. A borrower refinances a 10 percent, $60,000 mortgage with a 9 percent loan. Total refinance costs add up to $2,900. Rather than asking for these costs in cash, the lender adds them onto the loan amount, making the balance $62,900.

Example. The same borrower may elect to pay the refinance costs in cash at the time the refinanced loan is approved. The 10 percent loan is reduced to 9 percent, and the amount due in unchanged. However, the borrower had to pay $2,900 in cash to the lender.

A comparison of the monthly cost and total interest, based on a 15-year term at 9 percent, reveals the following data:

	$62,900 Loan	$60,000 Loan
Monthly payment	$ 637.98	$ 608.56
Difference	29.42	
Total interest	51,936	49,541
Difference	2,395	

When the additional interest is added to the amount of refinancing costs, the total difference between the two alternatives is $5,295 ($2,900 + $2,395).

THE BREAKEVEN POINT

You can save money by paying refinancing costs to the lender at the time the new loan is finalized. But as a practical matter, the money is not always going to be available. Whether you prepay these expenses or add to the amount of your debt, the value of refinancing should be evaluated in terms of how long it will take to offset the costs.

You know that you'll save money over the remainder of your repayment term, just because the interest rate is lower. You can even take out cash in some circumstances, reduce the repayment term, and still accelerate. But to truly compare terms of one refinance deal over another, figure out how long it takes to offset the cost of refinancing.

The total refinancing cost, divided by the savings in your monthly payment, equals the breakeven point. So if your total refinance costs are $2,400 and you will reduce your monthly payment by $76, it will take about 32 months to absorb that cost, or to break even:

$$\frac{\$2{,}400}{\$76 \text{ per month}} = 31.6 \text{ months}$$

This calculation is important if you plan to stay in your home for a limited number of years. In some cases, refinancing will not be profitable, even when you can get a lower interest rate.

Example. A homeowner plans to sell his home in two years. He can refinance his 13 percent mortgage with a 12 percent loan today. However, this refinancing will involve $2,400 in closing costs and will reduce monthly payments by $76. It would take 32 months to break even, so refinancing won't make sense.

Based on an $80,000 loan originally written with a 30-year term at 13 percent, monthly payments will equal $885 per month. Various refinance rates, monthly savings, and the breakeven months are shown in Figure 10–2.

The greater the reduction in interest rates by refinancing, the higher the monthly savings—and the shorter the breakeven time. However, if you use the strategy of leaving your monthly payment at the same level (thus accelerating to reduce the repayment term and interest expense), the breakeven point should be calculated differently.

Example. A homeowner is currently paying $885 per month on an original loan of $80,000 at 13 percent and with a 30-year term. Today, the balance is $65,000. The loan can be refinanced at 9 percent and will involve costs of $2,400. If payments are left

END OF 15TH YEAR:	
loan balance	$65,000
refinance costs	2,400
new balance	$67,400

	15-YEAR TERM:		
refinance rate	monthly payment	monthly savings	breakeven months
12%	$809	$ 76	32
11	766	119	20
10	724	161	15
9	684	201	12
8	644	241	10

Figure 10–2 Breakeven months. Original loan: $80,000, 30-year term, 13%, monthly payment of $885

at the same level, the loan will be repaid in 10 years. That's a repayment term five years less than the original, for a total savings of $52,884—compared to refinance costs of $2,400, or a profit of $50,484. Since the loan will be repaid in 10 years, the average profit from acceleration equals $5,048 per year.

This method is not truly accurate, since interest expenses are not equal each year and because the refinance costs must be paid in one sum, at the beginning of the loan term. However, to compare one refinancing plan to another, the calculation of average yearly savings net of closing costs is valid.

REFINANCING FOR HOME IMPROVEMENTS

You can refinance to pay for home improvements in one of two ways: by extending the term at the same rate you're now paying or by replacing your loan at a lower rate. In either case, you can plan your repayment schedule so that your monthly payment does not change.

Home improvement is a popular way to increase living space, maintain property, and improve life-style, all without having to move. And homeowners can fund those improvements by borrowing their equity with a second mortgage, or they can coordinate the timing of an improvement with favorable reductions in interest rates.

Example. A homeowner wants to invest $20,000 in improvements. The first mortgage had a balance of $80,000 and was written for a 30-year term with 10 percent interest. Twenty years later, the balance is $53,000.

This homeowner may be able to rewrite the loan at the same 10 percent rate or may find that a new loan can be taken out at a lower rate.

10% Example

The homeowner wants to replace a $53,000 debt with a $73,000 debt. For monthly payments of $704.48, the debt can be repaid in 20 years. In comparison, the original loan has 10 years to go. To pay off the entire balance in 10 years, monthly payments must be increased to $964.68, or $263 higher than payments being made on the original loan.

9% Example

The repayment of a $73,000 loan at 9 percent, with monthly payments of $699.94, will take 17 years. To repay within the original 10-year term, the monthly payment must be $924.75, or $223 more per month than is being paid on the original loan.

The decision about refinanced mortgages must be made in consideration of what you can afford to pay each month, balanced against the long-term cost of interest.

If you refinance strictly to take advantage of lower rates, you must be sure your break-even point occurs before you plan to move—or the decision will not save you money. But if you refinance to afford home improvements, you must plan for higher payments or for a longer repayment term and higher interest expense.

In the next chapter, we will discuss the dangers of mismanaging home equity, ways to identify common mortgage traps, and the proper use of equity lines of credit.

11 MANAGING YOUR DEBT

The purpose of accelerating mortgage debt is to reduce the total cost of your home. With interest added to the purchase price—even on an after-tax basis—you have considerable control over that cost. But the benefits of acceleration go beyond the price alone.

In this chapter, the importance of managing and preplanning debt is discussed. We will cover four major areas:

1. The careful selection and control of the acceleration and debt strategy, as part of your personal financial plan
2. The benefits and dangers of equity lines of credit
3. Acceleration strategies when your home's value is not rising
4. Building home equity to subsidize rent after you sell your home

ACHIEVING FINANCIAL FREEDOM

By selecting the date in the future that you will become free of monthly mortgage payments, you take control over your debt. If your reason for accelerating is to lower the cost of housing, then a second reason must be to take control of your budget.

Everyone defines financial success in his or her own way. To some, it means having a large sum of money. You might consider yourself successful once you build your investment and savings portfolio to $100,000 or more. But if, at the same time, you remain committed to a high level of monthly expense payments, you must also continue to earn a high level of income, just to meet your obligations.

To others, success means the elimination of recurring debt and monthly expenses. At the point that your income is much greater than your monthly commitments, you achieve the freedom to accumulate investments, increase leisure activities, choose the number of hours you will dedicate to work, and decide when to retire. In other words, success can be equated with the freedom to make choices.

With mortgage acceleration, you pick the date on which your mortgage will be paid off. At that point, you will be able to reduce your monthly budget, by doing away with the payment to a lender. For most people, the mortgage payment is the largest single obligation in the budget; once gone, families suddenly have flexibility and choices.

Working full time is more pleasurable when it's done by choice rather than by necessity. Without a mortgage payment, you have the choice to continue working a 40-hour week. Many people will choose to reduce their hours, go into their own business, or retire altogether. Others may continue working and save a larger portion of their take-home pay or use it to buy the things they've wanted for many years.

Example. One family accelerated their mortgage so that the debt was eliminated in 20 years rather than 30. The family members had wanted to start their own small business for many years but concluded that it would be too risky as long as they were obligated to repay a lender every month. Now, with a minimum monthly budget and full equity in their home, this family had the freedom to choose.

Any financial goal can be achieved with careful planning. To start your own small business, for example, you must evaluate your family's minimum needs versus your likely income. Starting a new business means a period of uncertainty. As long as you owe money on your mortgage, the risks of starting that business are substantially higher. But when that debt has been completely eliminated, you have many more choices. It will be easier to attain success in the business.

The same argument applies to retirement. You might decide it would be desirable to retire in 15 years, but you will owe money to a lender for the next 22 years. By accelerating so that the debt will be paid off by your target date, it will be easier to achieve your financial goal.

You can consider acceleration an end in itself, a way to reduce the cost of your home and own your property free and clear, or you can see it as the means for achieving other goals in a shorter period of time.

Example. With a 30-year mortgage of $80,000 at 10 percent interest, you will owe $74,826 at the end of the eighth year. If you would like to repay that debt in 15 years from that point, you must accelerate your required payment from $702.06 to $804.09 per month.

To calculate the required payment for any rate of interest and for any number of years, refer to the amortization table in the first appendix. Locate the column for the rate you are paying on your mortgage. Then find the line for the number of years in which you would like to repay your loan. Multiply the factor by the current balance of your loan to find the monthly payment.

THE PAYOFF DATE AND YOUR BUDGET

The selection of a payoff date for your mortgage must be coordinated with your personal financial plan and must be determined within the limits of your monthly budget. Using the amortization tables, you can compare various payoff dates for different years.

This comparison applies whether you are looking ahead to retirement or to any other personal goal. Figure 11–1 shows how a full mortgage term must be compared to a shorter target date in the future and also shows the degree of acceleration required to meet that goal.

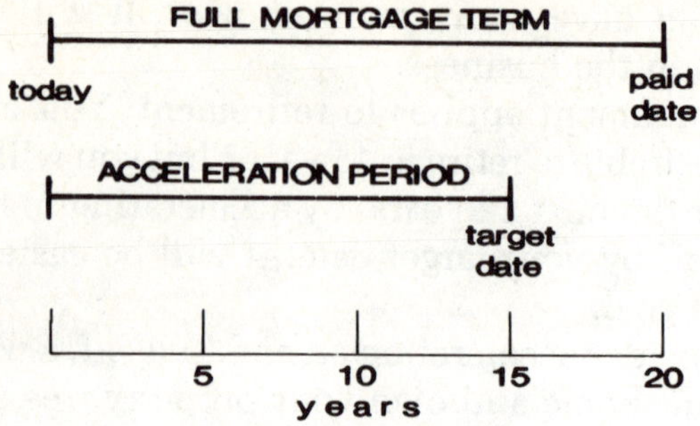

Figure 11–1 Target date

Example. Your original plan called for paying off your mortgage within 15 years. However, you decide that you cannot afford the higher payment and must modify your plan, taking one of the following actions:

1. Delay your payoff date so that current payments will be affordable. If, in the future, your income increases so that a greater rate of acceleration is possible, you can again modify the plan.
2. Tighten your family budget so that the original target date can be met. That will require spending less money elsewhere or doing away with other debts.
3. Increase your current income so that the original target date can be achieved. This action might require taking a second job or having a nonworking spouse go to work, at least temporarily.

Make your action decision based on how important it is to reach your target. You might be willing to delay the date of full repayment, rather than increasing monthly payments today. Or the goal might be so important that you're willing to work harder or spend less now.

No plans you make today will be permanent. Your plan must be flexible based on ever-changing obligations and income. Evaluate your ultimate goals (early retirement or starting your own business, for example) in the context of what you know and assume today and then change your plan as circumstances evolve.

Example. You owe $74,826 at the end of the eighth year in your 30-year mortgage term. You can select a payoff date by referring to the amortization tables for 10 percent interest. If the $804.09 payment necessary to repay the debt in 15 years is too high, you can check other repayment terms:

Years	Factor	Amount	Increase
16	.0104590	$782.61	$80.55
17	.0102121	764.13	62.07
18	.0099984	748.14	46.08
19	.0098126	734.24	32.18
20	.0096502	722.09	20.03

The coordination of goals and current resources is essential if your plan is to work. On the one hand, it is highly desirable to eliminate mortgage debt, so that your monthly budget requirement will be lower. On the other hand, you must devise a plan that works within today's budget.

The process is one of compromise. If you can afford to increase today's payment by $46 per month, you can reach your goal in 18 years; if you can increase acceleration to $62 per month, the debt will be eliminated in 17 years. Coordinate what you are *able* to pay today with the number of years you are *willing* to wait until you reach your goal.

Example. One family could not afford to accelerate its mortgage at a rate that would pay it off in 15 years. The family evaluated the amounts required for 16- through 20-year acceleration rates. The issue was one of affordability versus the importance of reaching a financial goal. The family had to compare what its budget could stand, recognizing that the lower the payment, the longer the delay in eliminating the debt.

The family members determined that the goal was so important that they had to reach their 15-year target. They needed to make an additional payment of $102.03 per month to eliminate their debt within 15 years. One spouse took a second job one evening per week, increasing the family's current income. That enabled them to meet their target date.

THE EQUITY LINE OF CREDIT

Some families arrive at a plan for repayment of their mortgage debt only to find that their debt becomes perpetual. This problem is likely to arise if you are one of the many people attracted to an equity line of credit.

Example. You are repaying your mortgage on an accelerated schedule, but you also have a line of credit secured by home equity. By your target date, you are still in debt and have many years to go until it will be repaid.

The equity line of credit is a great convenience or a great pitfall to building equity, all depending on how disciplined you are in using it. The typical line of credit agreement includes these terms:

1. You are granted a line of credit up to a specified percentage of the equity in your home.
2. You may draw against that line at any time you want and for any purpose.
3. The required monthly repayment will be for interest only, with principal due at the end of a specified term.

Example. Your home is valued at $125,000, and you owe approximately $65,000 on your current mortgage. A lender grants you an equity line of credit of $35,000, figured on 80 percent of available equity:

80% equity	$100,000
Less: Mortgage debt	65,000
Line of credit	$ 35,000

The effective interest rate will be 11 percent, so that the monthly payment will be calculated as 11 percent of the amount you have used against the total line of credit.

You are given a checkbook and can use the line of credit whenever you like, spending up to $35,000. The terms state that you will be required to make monthly repayments for interest only and that the entire amount will be due and payable in 10 years. So your monthly payment will depend on how much you use:

Amount Used	Monthly Payment
$ 5,000	$ 45.83
15,000	137.50
25,000	229.17
35,000	320.83

The problem with making interest-only payments is that at the end of the term you will still owe the full amount borrowed, and it will have to be repaid in one sum. For many people, that will mean having to refinance the debt with a traditional mortgage. If you have a line of credit, you might end up undoing the best of plans you make today by accumulating debt through your line of credit.

Example. Your goal is to pay off your $80,000 mortgage within 15 years. You accelerate monthly payments to achieve that goal. But at the same time, you contract with a lender for a 10-year line of credit, with a $35,000 maximum. By the 10th year, you have reached the $35,000 maximum, and that amount is now due. At that point, you still owe $40,460 on your $80,000 mortgage, so that your total debt is now $75,460. With only five years to go on your original deadline, your debt is nearly as high as the amount you borrowed through your first mortgage.

Misuse of an equity line of credit will keep you in debt and subvert your personal financial plan. A line of credit can serve as an excellent planning tool, but only if it's properly managed with these rules:

1. You must control the uses of the equity line of credit, so that you do not go into debt beyond the level you intend. This rule is where most people with lines of credit go wrong. If you intend to use that line only for home improvements and you can stick to that plan, then chances are your home's value will be increased by the amount of debt you accumulate. But it's also

tempting to repay credit card charges, buy a new car, or take a vacation, all funded with the line of credit. When that happens, your debt level increases, and the monthly interest payments grow as well.

2. You must make repayments on a schedule above interest only, so that the debt is reduced over time. Doing this eliminates the shock of having to refinance at the end of the term.

This rule will reduce the monthly interest level and will also help you avoid the need to refinance. The final balloon payment required in many equity line of credit agreements can come as an unexpected surprise if you do not plan ahead. And, since many lines of credit are based on adjustable rather than fixed interest rates, a preplanned level of repayment also helps you to control the cost of borrowing.

3. Because the line of credit is secured by an important family asset—your home—it should be used *only* in ways that increase home equity.

This rule will determine whether you invest or spend borrowed money. The equity line of credit is secured by the value of your home. When you use that line to pay off other debts, take vacations, or buy a car, you are converting a personal asset, the equity in your home, to spending. That's contrary to the purpose most people have in buying a home, which is to build security and value through direct ownership.

In contrast, a carefully controlled line of credit can be used to finance improvements, increasing the value of your home. As long as the debt level itself is controlled and repaid on a strict schedule, you will benefit from the equity line of credit.

Another appropriate use of the line of credit is to reduce the interest rate on an existing loan. Just as refinancing to reduce your effective rate is a smart move that saves money over time, the equity line of credit can be used to save money and to accelerate without increasing monthly payments.

Example. One family had an existing mortgage at 12.75 percent and a balance of $42,000. The repayment term on the original $48,000 loan was 15 years, and the monthly payment was $599.45. The mortgage was being repaid at the accelerated rate of $700 per month.

The family wanted to spend approximately $20,000 in home improvements, including all-new insulated windows, a new kitchen, a sliding glass door, an outside deck, and central air conditioning. But they also wanted to borrow the money without increasing their monthly payments.

The same lender offered an equity line of credit at the fixed rate of 11 percent, with interest-only monthly payments and a repayment date of 15 years. The lender was willing to give the homeowner a total line of $75,000. There was no prepayment penalty, and total closing costs, including two points, added up to $2,500.

The initial use of the line of credit was to pay off the previous loan and absorb the closing costs. While the lender was accepting a lower rate of interest, the trade-off was not a total loss. The lender not only received two points for the conversion but could increase the debt to $75,000—meaning more interest over the 15-year term.

Once the line of credit was approved, the debt became $44,500 (the previous loan's balance of $42,000 plus closing costs of $2,500). The initial required monthly payment was $407.92 (11 percent interest). The family made a $700 payment, which would repay the total debt in slightly more than eight years. However, with the additional spending the family planned, that picture would change.

Over the next few months, the family did spend $20,000 more from their line of credit for home improvements. With the accelerated repayment schedule and the additional use of the line of credit, the following activity occurred:

Month	Amount Spent	Interest Paid	Principal Paid	Balance
				$44,500.00
1	$ 0	$407.92	$292.08	44,207.92
2	9,000	487.74	212.26	52,995.66
3	4,000	522.46	177.54	56,818.12
4	3,000	548.33	151.67	56,666.45
5	4,000	556.11	143.89	60,522.56
6	0	554.79	145.21	60,377.35
7	0	553.46	146.54	60,230.81
8	0	552.12	147.88	60,082.93

With the continuing payment of $700 per month, the balance of this loan will be repaid in slightly more than 14 years. Thus, the line of credit will have enabled this family to make its $20,000 in home improvements with

No increase in its monthly payment

Repayment of the line of credit within 15 years and with no balloon payment at the end of the term

With careful planning and some shopping for rates and terms, you might be able to find a lender who will offer similar terms. By controlling your level of debt and by following a plan of acceleration, you could maintain the same level of payments in a similar manner.

The danger, of course, is that the full line of credit is available. In the example above, the family could spend up to $75,000 at any time it wished. But that would change the plan. To make repayment by its scheduled date, the family would have to increase monthly payments.

You can benefit from the controlled and planned use of a line of credit. But if you cannot discipline yourself to avoid excessive spending, you will increase debt rather than eliminate it. In that situation, you convert your home equity to the lender in the form of excessive interest and counteract your plan to build value over time.

WHEN YOUR HOME'S VALUE IS NOT RISING

The selection of a repayment date is tied in with your personal financial plan, and an equity line of credit can be advantageous or highly dangerous. But any form of acceleration and debt control should also be evaluated when your home's value is not rising.

You might accept the value of an acceleration plan if the assumption is that a home's value will rise over time but reject the strategy if your home's value is falling. But even in a depressed market, acceleration is still a sound idea.

One argument against acceleration goes as follows: "Paying off your mortgage more rapidly is a smart idea as long as your home's market value is rising. But if your home's value is falling, you're throwing good money after bad."

The flaw in this argument is that it assumes a point of view of an investor, not that of a homeowner. It's true that if you make a poor investment in the stock market, it may be unwise to continue putting more money into the same stock. But with your own home, you must remember that the majority of your purchase is represented by debt and that you are buying personal security, not just investment value.

In an extreme case, a family can simply walk away from a home that has fallen in value. However, that would also mean consequences to the family's credit rating. For example, a family purchases a home for $100,000 and finances 80 percent. Five years later, its mortgage debt is still more than $77,000, but the home's value has fallen to $75,000. The 20 percent down payment is lost, and the market value is lower than the amount of debt.

In this extreme situation, the family could simply accept its loss and move elsewhere. The lender would foreclose the mortgage and sell the home at the best price it could get.

This family will still need a place to live and will probably have to rent an apartment or house. If the family attempts to borrow money to buy another home in the near future, it will be extremely difficult to find a lender who will approve the loan. It's more likely that the family will stay in its depreciated home and continue to make mortgage payments.

The continuing need for shelter makes your home more than an investment. Thus, the value goes beyond current market value. Assuming you can afford the monthly payment to which you are committed, you probably plan to keep your home for many years.

Your mortgage debt will continue until it is paid off, regardless of what happens to your home's market value. By keeping in mind that the amount you pay in interest ultimately determines the true cost of your home, acceleration makes sense, whether market values rise or fall.

Example. Your $100,000 home will cost you $252,735 if an $80,000 debt is paid off at 10 percent interest in 30 years. You can reduce that cost to $154,744 by repaying the mortgage over 15 years. These facts remain unchanged regardless of that home's value after the mortgage has been repaid.

The purpose of acceleration is to reduce interest and the total cost of your home, building equity more rapidly. That $100,000 home may double in value, stay the same, or even fall. As long as you are an owner and not a seller, acceleration continues to save you money.

A SEPARATE ISSUE

The problem of depreciated market value is completely separate from the question of acceleration. If you select a home in an area where employment falls off and where demand disappears, values will not rise. But even if that occurs, you must still be concerned with the effects of interest rather than with sales value.

Example. You repay your $80,000 mortgage at an accelerated 15-year rate, reducing interest costs by $97,991 over the 30-year required term. You then sell your home, which has a market value of only $85,000. You will receive $85,000, less closing costs. As an investment, the outcome would be

Sales price	$ 85,000
Less: Total payments	154,744
Loss	$ −69,744

If you had made payments at the 30-year rate, you would still owe $65,330 at the end of the 15th year and upon sale at $85,000 would receive cash of only $19,670 (less closing costs). As an investment, the outcome would be

Sales price	$ 85,000
Less: Total payments	126,371
Loss	$ −41,371

By not accelerating, the investment loss would be $28,373 less ($69,744 less $41,371). So it appears that when a home's value declines, acceleration would be a poor idea. However, the evaluation must consider both the investment loss and the cash proceeds upon sale:

	15 Years	30 Years
Total payments	$154,744	$126,371
Sales price	85,000	85,000
Loss	$ 69,744	$ 41,371
Difference	−28,373	
Cash at sale	$ 85,000	$ 19,670
Difference	+65,330	

The possibility that your home could decline in value is an inescapable risk of purchase. That risk cannot be anticipated in every case, since today's economic conditions could change drastically during the time you own your home. The best you can do is reduce that risk by buying in areas that hold great promise for future market value.

A decline in value does not offset the intrinsic value of acceleration. Acceleration reduces the *cost* of your home by building equity and reducing interest expense. The question of market value becomes a concern at the point that you become a seller. With acceleration, you will have greater equity in your home, represented by the lower level of debt. That means more cash in hand after the sale, no matter what the market value at that time.

If you plan to repurchase in the same area, a depressed market value for your home will also be reflected in prices of other homes. That means a lower repurchase price; you still benefit from acceleration and greater cash upon sale. This argument is the same when prices have risen.

Example. You sell your home that cost $100,000 at a market price of $85,000. Other comparable homes in the same area are also worth $85,000.

Example. You sell your home that cost $100,000 at a market price of $150,000. Other comparable homes in the same area are also worth $150,000.

Market values do not change in isolation. Prices will rise and fall in the same direction, so that selling one home and buying another at a similar price does not affect the overall value of your investment. The only way you can *control* the cost of your home is by accelerating your debt. Ultimately, you only "take out" equity when you sell a home and do not repurchase. At that point, you will profit from any acceleration practiced over the years, as well as from increased market values. And if homes have fallen in value, you will then suffer the consequences of those lower values.

EQUITY TO SUBSIDIZE RENT

No one wants to purchase a home that falls in value. But if you plan to remain in your present home for many years, you should not be overly concerned with ultimate investment value. You cannot control the market, but you can control your cost of your home.

Chances are that, over the long term, values of residential real estate will continue to rise. This trend has been true historically, since real estate is a limited commodity. If you live in an area where the population is increasing, where companies are hiring, and where the economy is strong, it is likely that your home's market value will grow in time. You may eventually take out your equity and put it to other use, assuming you no longer need to own a home.

Equity comes from two primary sources. First is increase in demand and a growth in the market value of homes like yours; second is the accumulation of equity through monthly payments to your lender. Once you own your home free and clear, you can sell your home and become a renter, taking a large amount of cash out of your property investment at the same time.

While a final sale is generally taxable, you benefit from two provisions in tax law. First is the rule that you defer profits from selling your home as long as you buy or build another home within two years. If the value of your new home is equal to or greater than the home you sold, all profits are deferred, and you are not taxed. If the new home's value is lower than the home you sold, you are taxed on the difference.

Example. You purchased a home for $100,000 eight years ago and sell it this year for $125,000. You buy a new home within two years for $130,000. You will not be taxed on any of your profits.

Example. You purchased a home for $100,000 eight years ago and sell it this year for $125,000. You buy a new home within two years for $118,000. The difference between sales and purchase price, $7,000, is taxable. The rest of your $25,000 profit is deferred.

A second provision of the tax law is that as much as $125,000 of profits are completely excluded from tax for sellers aged 55 or older. This provision is allowed only once. But added to the deferral benefit, it means that you could own a series of homes over your lifetime and never be taxed on any of your profits.

This benefit becomes valuable if you decide to sell your home and become a renter. For example, if you receive $125,000, representing the full equity in your home, you would have to pay $35,000 in federal taxes if your effective rate were 28 percent. That leaves only $90,000 in after-tax equity.

As part of your retirement plan, you can look ahead to selling your home once it's owned free and clear and using your equity to subsidize rental payments. By accelerating your mortgage today, you will be in control of the date of repayment and can determine and plan your retirement age.

Example. At the age of 35, a couple enters a 30-year mortgage on their $100,000 home, financing $80,000 at 10 percent. Monthly payments are $702.06. Ten years later, husband and wife agree to retire within 15 years, when both will be 60. However, a major problem with this plan is that they will still owe their lender for five years of payments. To make their retirement practical, they would like to repay their mortgage in 15 years rather than 20.

This plan requires acceleration. Ten years into the 30-year

mortgage, the balance of the mortgage is $72,750. To repay that amount in 15 years, monthly payments must be increased to $781.78, or an increase of $79.72 per month.

The couple initiates their plan and pays off the mortgage by age 55. They then sell their home, and they receive $125,000 after all closing costs and commissions are paid. They then rent a small apartment and retire.

Because they use their once-in-a-lifetime exclusion, they are not taxed on their proceeds. And because they no longer need to make mortgage payments, they can live on much less per month. Finally, by investing their $125,000 proceeds, they can pay their rent from interest income. That's taxable, of course, but by reducing their monthly budget and, in the process, creating a supplemental income base, they can live comfortably on their combined interest and pension income.

The proceeds from a sale can be invested in a very conservative way, such as in an insured bank or savings account, in U.S. government securities, in short-term time accounts, or in higher-yielding but riskier mutual fund shares. Table 11–1 shows the average monthly interest on $125,000, assuming quarterly compounding.

In an insured account yielding only 5 percent, you will receive $521 per month. If you invest proceeds in certificates of deposit, government securities, or money market funds yielding 6 percent, the monthly amount rises to $625. And for slightly more risk, the effective rate and monthly income can be increased.

In the example of the couple that accelerated their payments to meet a 15-year repayment, the degree of budget relief, combined with additional interest income, makes a significant difference in the monthly budget:

Elimination of mortgage payments	$ 782
Interest income, 5%	521
Total budget relief per month	$1,303

In spite of claims made by lenders that you should "put your equity to work," you never really take out your profits except by selling your home and becoming a renter. When that day comes, you can then put your equity to work generating income for retirement.

Even if you plan to remain in your home after your mortgage has been paid in full, your budget can still be reduced because you no longer must continue to pay the lender. Whether you remain in your home or sell and become a renter, your personal financial goals can be reached more quickly and profits can be increased with a plan of acceleration.

In the final chapter, we will look at the problem of temptation in equity. All homeowners are under considerable pressure from lenders to take out their equity, through refinancing or lines of credit. You can avoid that temptation by identifying your goals and making decisions based on your personal financial plan.

Table 11-1 Interest income, $125,000 equity

Rate[a]	Monthly Interest
5%	$521
6	625
7	729
8	833

[a]Assuming quarterly compounding.

12 AVOIDING TEMPTATION

As a homeowner, you are constantly advised to put your equity to work, to not leave it idle in your home. The idea of accelerating your mortgage payments is said to be a poor idea, and ads promise big profits elsewhere, or the convenience of having cash in hand.

For the financial advisor who is paid by way of commissions, mortgage acceleration ties up your money and yields no profits. But when you can be convinced to borrow equity to invest elsewhere, that advisor will earn a commission. And for the lender, who earns a profit from interest, the more you borrow, the greater the long-term profits.

THE ARGUMENTS AGAINST ACCELERATION

A lot of energy is put into explaining why you should not accelerate your mortgage. Many of those who make the arguments against this idea are not trying to deceive you; they sincerely believe what they claim. But any true comparison will show that the arguments are flawed.

When lenders grant loans to homeowners secured by equity, their risks are very low or nonexistent. You are unlikely to walk away from a home in which you have built up considerable equity over the years or that has increased in market value since the time you purchased.

Commissioned salespeople are able to understand only the need to create funds to invest. Their emphasis is on the quality of investments they will recommend, and not on whether or not you should go into debt to a mortgage lender.

Example. A financial planner advises you to purchase shares in a mutual fund. Its track record shows substantial growth above market averages, and even when the overall market has been down, the fund lost less than the market as a whole. You are convinced that investing money in this fund would be prudent and profitable.

The problem, though, is that you have very little money available to invest. So the planner suggests that you refinance your mortgage. A plan is developed so that you can "free up" several thousand dollars and, at the same time, lower your monthly payment. Your existing mortgage ($80,000, 10 percent, 30-year term) has a current balance of $63,350, and you have 14 years to go before it will be paid in full.

The planner suggests you refinance to $75,000. Allowing for the cost of refinancing, that will free up about $10,000. And starting your 30-year term over again, your monthly payments (at 10 percent) will be $658.18, or about $44 lower than what you're paying today.

At first glance, this seems a sensible plan. Your monthly payments will be lower, and you free up $10,000 to invest. This tactic is popular among salespeople, because it seems to reduce your costs. In reality, though, it increases the cost of your home, as well as your risks. Keep in mind that

1. This plan will double the remaining cost of buying your home. On the original loan, the remaining 14 years of payments adds up to $118,719. Refinancing for a full 30-year term will cost you $236,945.

2. For the additional cost of more than $118,000, you are freeing up only $10,000 to invest. You are also increasing your repayment term by 16 years.

3. The past, by itself, is not a dependable indicator of investment performance. Investments with the best performance record might do poorly in the future. Thus, you assume a risk by converting home equity to an investment that could decline in value.

4. No matter how this plan is explained, it's still a form of borrowing money to invest. Would you seek a loan from your bank for this purpose if you didn't own a home?

5. Your home equity is illiquid and thus can be thought of as unavailable to you. But once you convert your equity into a more liquid investment, like a mutual fund, it will be easier to sell off shares and spend that money elsewhere.

Never look only at the immediate benefits of borrowing money. It's true that you can free up cash while reducing your monthly cost, but that's deceptive. A true comparison will include an evaluation of the total cost of borrowing money.

KEEPING YOUR PERSPECTIVE

Recognize that the arguments against acceleration often are self-serving. The lender or salesperson gets no income when you invest in your own home. Always compare costs in the long term, and always question the logic of increasing your debt and repayment term.

Acceleration is a means for controlling the total cost of your home. By building equity as rapidly as you can afford, you decrease the interest expense of your mortgage and reduce that cost. Salespeople argue that equity left untapped is idle, a point that appeals to guilt. But it's a mistake to assume that advisors know more than you about financial matters or that they have access to secrets or formulas for wealth and investing success. The truth is, they may understand the attributes of investment products, but as often as not, they know very little about risk.

Example. An advisor recommends an investment, claiming that it is low-risk. That claim is based on the conservative nature of the investment. However, the question of *your* risks is never raised. When you borrow money secured by home equity, you assume a substantial risk, by putting your home and your family's security on the line. Any argument in favor of an investment that is based only on outside risks misses the point entirely.

Be aware of your personal risks whenever you are approached, directly or through advertisements, and told that your equity is idle. Compare the cost of borrowing and the need to make monthly payments for many years to come to the apparent value of an investment. If you are willing to assume those risks, you certainly have the freedom to borrow money, but first compare costs and then compare yields and risks.

In comparing the cost of borrowing to likely yields from other investments, you will discover that you are probably better off building equity, rather than spending or investing it. If your mortgage rate is 10 percent, you must be able to find an outside investment that matches that, just to break even. And the risk of equity building is extremely low. Be aware of the added risk in investing elsewhere, even when you can get a higher return on your money.

Example. You are paying 10 percent on your mortgage. A financial planner suggests you refinance to free up funds, which can be invested currently at a 13 percent yield.

To evaluate this idea realistically, you should be aware of these points:

1. For the increase in yield of 3 percent, you will probably be assuming substantially greater risks than you have by building equity.
2. If you refinance, your monthly payment will increase, or the term of your loan will have to be extended beyond your current repayment date.
3. There is probably no guarantee that the current 13 percent rate will continue beyond the first year. It's more likely that in the future that rate will change. But your mortgage rate is set for the entire term.
4. If any tax arguments are made as part of the argument, remember that the yield on your investment will be taxable. So higher deductions will be offset by higher taxable income.

MORTGAGE MANAGEMENT RULES

To keep your perspective on the value of acceleration as part of your personal financial plan, attend closely to the following 10 rules.

Compare Equity Building to Other Investments

Always make your comparison with three important points in mind: yield versus cost, risk, and liquidity.

The yield from an investment must be compared to the cost of a mortgage, not only for the immediate year but for the entire mortgage term. So a rate of return that's guaranteed for one year will not always remain as high in the future. But your mortgage rate will always be the same (or, in the case of an adjustable-rate mortgage, it will rise).

You can control the cost of your home by beginning a plan of acceleration. How does that compare to an outside investment? Chances are you will conclude that the best investment you can make will be in reducing interest on your mortgage and building equity as quickly as your budget will allow.

Mortgage acceleration is a very illiquid investment, because you can get the money back only by again going into debt. It can be a disadvantage if you begin a program with funds you will need later. And it can be an advantage because that money is not easily taken out and misused for other reasons.

Design a Plan to Suit Your Budget

No financial plan is practical if it works only on paper. It must work within the context of what your budget can bear. If you can afford only a modest amount today, the schedule can be revised later, when your income increases.

One of the major benefits of designing your own plan is flexibility. You can increase or decrease payments according to changing financial circumstances and prospects. The ability to modify your plan as often as you like makes acceleration one of the most flexible ways you can invest.

Establish Your Emergency Reserve Fund before You Begin an Acceleration Plan

Acceleration will save you thousands of dollars over the years and will reduce the term required to own your home free and clear. But because the money you invest in equity is not easily taken back, you must first put aside enough money to take care of emergencies, like losing your job.

Once your emergency reserve plan has been established, acceleration makes sense. But don't overlook the critical importance of liquidity as a first priority.

Be Aware of the Motives of People Who Advise You

Lenders are in the business of charging interest on borrowed money, and salespeople earn their living from commissions. Both of these groups are naturally opposed to acceleration. It decreases the lender's overall income from interest and yields nothing for the financial advisor.

The lender's risks are low with secured loans. A mortgage is secured by the equity in your home and is a very low-risk loan from the lender's point of view. And salespeople have absolutely no risk in advising you to refinance or take out a second mortgage. They are motivated to create money for investment, and the greater the amount, the higher their commissions.

Don't View Equity as "Idle" Money

Equity is value, and the only way you can truly take it out of your home is by selling and not purchasing another home. If you buy a less expensive property, you will take out some of your equity when you sell, and if you become a renter, you will take it all. But as long as you live in your home, you can control the total cost based on how rapidly you pay your mortgage debt.

The argument that your equity is sitting idle in your home is deceptive. It implies that you are somehow mismanaging your finances when, in fact, the cost of compounded interest can drastically raise the cost of your home. Don't forget that "taking out your equity" really means borrowing money.

Make a Clear Distinction Between Assets and Income

Assets, like your home, should be insured, maintained, and increased in value. Build equity in your assets, and spend only your income. When you borrow money secured by home equity, you are converting an asset rather than making it grow. If that money is used to add to your home, then it's reinvested. But if it's used to buy a car or to take a vacation or spent in any other way, then you increase debt and reduce equity.

Decide to spend your income and not the equity in your home. If you want to invest, start a plan for putting a specific amount of each paycheck into a mutual fund or some other investment, but resist the arguments favoring taking out your equity.

Don't Worry about Market Value until You're Ready to Sell Your Home

One popular argument against acceleration is that it makes no sense when the value of your home is falling. A more realistic point of view is that you are obligated to repay your mortgage no matter what is happening to market value. Acceleration reduces the long-term cost of that mortgage loan and makes sense even when market value is falling.

Market value is relative. If you sell your home and buy another one in the same area, you will have to pay the same approximate price for a similar home. If your home's value has doubled since you purchased it, then so have the prices of similar homes. And if your home's market value has declined, then other homes in the area have fallen in value as well. In the event you did sell and move, the relative market value is not as critical as many homeowners believe.

Resist viewing your home for its investment value. As long as you can afford the mortgage payment to which you have committed yourself, the decision you have to make is whether or not to accelerate payments. The question of market value should not affect that decision.

Don't Be Swayed by a Need for Tax Deductions

Critics of mortgage acceleration like to point to the value of deducting mortgage interest. But the argument is a flawed one. You are always better off paying a lower amount of interest and deducting less, no matter what tax rate you use.

Make comparisons on an after-tax basis and be sure the comparison is a valid one. Don't compare after-tax interest costs to before-tax yields on other investments. And don't fall for the popular argument that high deductions are more desirable than lower interest costs.

Refinance Your Mortgage Only When It Makes Sense Financially

If you refinance to free up money, you will either have to pay more each month or extend the repayment term. In either case, it's expensive. However, there are two conditions when refinancing makes sense. First is when it reduces interest costs over time; second is when the money you receive upon refinancing is used to improve your family's living space and comfort.

A reduction in interest rates is the best reason to refinance. A lower rate will mean lower monthly payments. Or if you continue paying at the same level as the higher interest rate, it means acceleration without changing your monthly budget. The cost of refinancing will be absorbed by the savings created with the lower rate.

A major advantage of home ownership is that improvements can be financed through equity—and those improvements add comfort and enjoyment for your family while increasing market value. You can refinance or take out a second mortgage to pay for additions, as an alternative to moving, and fund those improvements with your existing home equity.

Be Aware of Both Interest Savings and Repayment Date When Comparing Acceleration Plans

There are two aspects to consider when comparing different acceleration plans: the total savings in interest and the repayment date.

The amount you save in interest represents a reduction in the cost of buying your home. The greater the acceleration rate, the more you save. And the earlier your repayment date, the sooner your budget can be reduced for permanent monthly expenses. Your plan translates to a comfortable retirement, an earlier start for other investments, or an improvement in your life-style.

An additional benefit of rapid acceleration is the increase in future borrowing power. The greater your equity, the higher the amount you can borrow in later years. If you view home equity as a source for secured debt, then acceleration makes sense as a means for building equity for that purpose.

YOUR OWN DECISION

Many homeowners accept the high cost of financing their homes as inevitable and unavoidable. Many have been told that acceleration is a bad idea, so they do not take the steps to reduce the cost of their home. Many others are not aware of the significant savings they can create with a self-designed plan and budget.

You can control your total interest expense to a high degree, even on a limited budget. On average, for example, a $25 addition to your monthly payment will take five years off a 30-year term. That's a lot of savings for a very small monthly investment.

Once you know how much can be saved by starting your own acceleration plan, and as long as that plan is designed with your budget in mind, you will be in control. You can reach future goals for full ownership of your home by a specific year and for an overall reduction in interest costs. The plan you design today can be changed in the future, as your financial status changes—

even to the point that acceleration is increased substantially over the initial level you select.

Outside advisors—loan officers and financial planners, for example—can serve as knowledgeable sources of information and might even suggest ways to increase your net worth and manage your money. But their perspectives about mortgage acceleration are likely to be distorted by their own circumstances. Keep this in mind whenever you receive advice about managing your mortgage.

Based on whether or not you accelerate payments, that cost can vary by $100,000 or even more. You do not have to pay the high interest that's built into your mortgage term. Every dollar you invest today shortens that term and lowers the cost of your home. If owning a home is one of your highest goals, then you must also be concerned with the cost of reaching that goal. And the most satisfying discovery you can make is that the cost of your goal is within your control.

APPENDIX 1 AMORTIZATION TABLES

Loan amortization tables report the amount of money that must be paid to a lender each month to repay a loan by the end of a specific term. There are three factors at work in determining this monthly payment:

The interest rate
The amount borrowed
The term of years

All three factors will determine the actual amount required to repay the loan. The higher the interest rate and amount borrowed and the shorter the term, the higher that recurring payment must be.

Amortization tables will further break down interest by the compounding method. Most mortgages are repaid with a monthly compounding of interest, meaning that the amount charged each month is equal to 1/12 of the annual rate.

Quarterly compounding would involve a quarterly payment at a rate of interest equal to one-fourth of the annual amount. Semiannual compounding would be figured at one-half the annual rate, with two payments per year.

The tables in this appendix are based on monthly compounding at various rates of interest. Amortization tables will be found in one of two forms. First is the type that lists the actual payment that must be made. At first glance, these tables are easier to use, because no additional computation is required.

The second type of table lists a factor for each year and each rate of interest. This factor is the amount required to amortize \$1. In order to figure the monthly payment, you must multiply the amount of the loan by the factor. With a little practice, this type of amortization is easier and more flexible to use, notably in comparing acceleration plans.

Example. Refer to the 10 percent table. The list of factors is given for each year. The last line is for amortization over a 30-year period, and the factor listed is .0087757. Multiply this factor times the amount of a loan to determine the monthly payment:

$$.0087757 \times \$80{,}000 = \$702.06$$

In considering a plan of acceleration, you might be interested in figuring the amount of monthly payment required for 25, 20, or 15 years. Locate the lines for those years, and multiply the factors:

1. 25 years:

$$.0090870 \times \$80{,}000 = \$726.96$$

2. 20 years:

$$.0096502 \times \$80{,}000 = \$772.02$$

3. 15 years:

$$.0107461 \times \$80{,}000 = \$859.69$$

The factor table is more convenient to use than a table that offers a monthly amount, due to the ease of computing payments on odd amounts of loans.

Example. Your current loan balance is $64,815. To compute the required monthly payment from a table that provides amounts per month, you will have to break down the loan amount into segments. Most amount tables show the monthly payment for loans at intervals of $1,000 or $5,000. So at 10 percent and with a 15-year term, the payment is estimated by breaking down the loan amount:

	Amount	Payment
	$60,000	$644.77
	4,000	42.99
	800	8.60
	10	.10
	5	.05
Total	$64,815	$696.51

The procedure with a factor table is much easier. Find the 15-year line for the 10 percent rate, and multiply the factor by the loan amount:

$$.0107461 \times \$64,815 = \$696.51$$

With the factor table, you can arrive at the same answer but are required to take only one step.

A third use of the factor table is to compute the required monthly payment when you are thinking of refinancing an existing loan at a lower rate of interest.

Example. Your original loan was for $80,000 and was amortized over 30 years at 12 percent. Monthly payments are $822.90. Now, with 18 years remaining, you owe $72,696 and are considering refinancing that loan at 10 percent. What will the monthly payment be for various repayment terms?

Solution. Refer to the 10 percent interest column, and multiply the factors for the years you want to evaluate by the current loan balance:

Years	Factor	Loan	Payment
12	.0119508	$72,696	$868.78
13	.0114785	72,696	834.44
14	.0110820	72,696	805.62
15	.0107461	72,696	781.20

The monthly repayment required for each term can now be compared to the current 12 percent loan, for which monthly payments are $822.90. By reducing the interest rate, monthly payments can be reduced, and the loan can be repaid in fewer years. But in order to make that comparison, the factor table is much easier to use than an amount amortization table.

In the following pages, amortization factors are given for interest rates at ¼ percent intervals between 8 and 15 percent.

Payments to Amortize 1 (Monthly Compounding)

Years	8%	8¼%	8½%	8¾%	9%	9¼%	Months
1	.0869884	.0871041	.0872198	.0873356	.0874515	.0875675	12
2	.0452273	.0453414	.0454557	.0455702	.0456847	.0457996	24
3	.0313364	.0314519	.0315675	.0316836	.0317997	.0319163	36
4	.0244129	.0245305	.0246483	.0247666	.0248850	.0250040	48
5	.0202764	.0203963	.0205165	.0206373	.0207584	.0208799	60
6	.0175332	.0176556	.0177784	.0179018	.0180255	.0181499	72
7	.0155862	.0157111	.0158365	.0159625	.0160891	.0162163	84
8	.0141367	.0142641	.0143921	.0145209	.0146502	.0147803	96
9	.0130187	.0131487	.0132794	.0134108	.0135429	.0136758	108
10	.0121328	.0122653	.0123986	.0125327	.0126676	.0128033	120
11	.0114154	.0115505	.0116864	.0118232	.0119608	.0120993	132
12	.0108245	.0109621	.0111006	.0112400	.0113803	.0115216	144
13	.0103307	.0104708	.0106118	.0107539	.0108968	.0110408	156
14	.0099132	.0100557	.0101992	.0103438	.0104894	.0106361	168
15	.0095565	.0097015	.0098474	.0099945	.0101427	.0102920	180
16	.0092493	.0093966	.0095449	.0096945	.0098452	.0099970	192
17	.0089826	.0091322	.0092829	.0094349	.0095880	.0097424	204
18	.0087496	.0089015	.0090546	.0092090	.0093644	.0095212	216
19	.0085450	.0086991	.0088545	.0090111	.0091690	.0093281	228
20	.0083644	.0085207	.0086782	.0088372	.0089973	.0091587	240
21	.0082043	.0083627	.0085224	.0086834	.0088458	.0090094	252
22	.0080618	.0082222	.0083841	.0085472	.0087117	.0088775	264
23	.0079345	.0080970	.0082609	.0084261	.0085927	.0087606	276
24	.0078205	.0079850	.0081508	.0083181	.0084866	.0086566	288
25	.0077182	.0078846	.0080523	.0082215	.0083920	.0085639	300
26	.0076260	.0077942	.0079638	.0081348	.0083072	.0084809	312
27	.0075428	.0077128	.0078842	.0080570	.0082313	.0084067	324
28	.0074675	.0076393	.0078124	.0079870	.0081630	.0083402	336
29	.0073994	.0075729	.0077477	.0079239	.0081016	.0082805	348
30	.0073376	.0075127	.0076891	.0078671	.0080462	.0082268	360

Payments to Amortize 1 (Monthly Compounding) (Continued)

Years	9½%	9¾%	10%	10¼%	10½%	10¾%	Months
1	.0876836	.0877997	.0879159	.0880323	.0881486	.0882651	12
2	.0459145	.0460297	.0461449	.0462604	.0463760	.0464919	24
3	.0320329	.0321500	.0322672	.0323847	.0325024	.0326205	36
4	.0251231	.0252427	.0253626	.0254829	.0256034	.0257243	48
5	.0210019	.0211243	.0212470	.0213703	.0214939	.0216180	60
6	.0182747	.0184001	.0185258	.0186522	.0187790	.0189063	72
7	.0163440	.0164723	.0166012	.0167307	.0168607	.0169913	84
8	.0149109	.0150423	.0151742	.0153068	.0154400	.0155740	96
9	.0138094	.0139437	.0140787	.0142145	.0143509	.0144881	108
10	.0129398	.0130771	.0132151	.0133540	.0134935	.0136339	120
11	.0122386	.0123789	.0125199	.0126618	.0128045	.0129480	132
12	.0116637	.0118069	.0119508	.0120957	.0122414	.0123881	144
13	.0111857	.0113317	.0114785	.0116263	.0117750	.0119247	156
14	.0107837	.0109324	.0110820	.0112327	.0113843	.0115370	168
15	.0104422	.0105937	.0107461	.0108996	.0110540	.0112095	180
16	.0101499	.0103040	.0104590	.0106152	.0107724	.0109307	192
17	.0098978	.0100544	.0102121	.0103710	.0105308	.0106918	204
18	.0096791	.0098383	.0099984	.0101599	.0103223	.0104859	216
19	.0094884	.0096500	.0098126	.0099765	.0101414	.0103075	228
20	.0093213	.0094852	.0096502	.0098165	.0099838	.0101523	240
21	.0091743	.0093405	.0095078	.0096763	.0098460	.0100168	252
22	.0090446	.0092129	.0093825	.0095532	.0097251	.0098981	264
23	.0089297	.0091002	.0092718	.0094447	.0096187	.0097938	276
24	.0088277	.0090002	.0091739	.0093488	.0095248	.0097020	288
25	.0087370	.0089114	.0090870	.0092639	.0094418	.0096210	300
26	.0086560	.0088322	.0090098	.0091885	.0093683	.095492	312
27	.0085836	.0087616	.0089410	.0091215	.0093030	.094857	324
28	.0085188	.0086985	.0088796	.0090618	.0092450	.094293	336
29	.0084607	.0086421	.0088248	.0090086	.0091934	.093793	348
30	.0084085	.0085916	.0087757	.0089611	.0091474	.0093349	360

Payments to Amortize 1 (Monthly Compounding) (Continued)

Years	11%	11¼%	11½%	11¾%	12%	12¼%	Months
1	.0883817	.0884984	.0886151	.0887319	.0888488	.0889658	12
2	.0466078	.0467240	.0468403	.0469569	.0470735	.0471904	24
3	.0327387	.0328573	.0329760	.0330951	.0332143	.0333339	36
4	.0258455	.0259671	.0260890	.0262113	.0263338	.0264568	48
5	.0217424	.0218674	.0219926	.0221184	.0222444	.0223710	60
6	.0190341	.0191624	.0192912	.0194205	.0195502	.0196805	72
7	.0171224	.0172542	.0173865	.0175194	.0176527	.0177868	84
8	.0157084	.0158436	.0159794	.0161158	.0162528	.0163906	96
9	.0146259	.0147645	.0149037	.0150437	.0151842	.0153256	108
10	.0137750	.0139169	.0140595	.0142030	.0143471	.0144920	120
11	.0130923	.0132376	.0133835	.0135303	.0136779	.0138263	132
12	.0125356	.0126840	.0128332	.0129833	.0131342	.0132860	144
13	.0120753	.0122268	.0123792	.0125325	.0126867	.0128418	156
14	.0116905	.0118451	.0120006	.0121570	.0123143	.0124726	168
15	.0113660	.0115235	.0116819	.0118414	.0120017	.0121630	180
16	.0110900	.0112504	.0114116	.0115740	.0117373	.0119016	192
17	.0108538	.0110169	.0111810	.0113461	.0115122	.0116793	204
18	.0106505	.0108163	.0109830	.0111508	.0113195	.0114893	216
19	.0104746	.0106429	.0108122	.0109826	.0111539	.0113262	228
20	.0103219	.0104926	.0106643	.0108371	.0110109	.0111857	240
21	.0101887	.0103617	.0105358	.0107109	.0108870	.0110641	252
22	.0100722	.0102475	.0104237	.0106011	.0107794	.0109587	264
23	.0099701	.0101474	.0103258	.0105052	.0106856	.0108670	276
24	.0098803	.0100596	.0102400	.0104214	.0106038	.0107872	288
25	.0098011	.0099824	.0101647	.0103480	.0105322	.0107175	300
26	.0097313	.0099144	.0100984	.0102834	.0104695	.0106565	312
27	.0096695	.0098543	.0100401	.0102268	.0104145	.0106031	324
28	.0096148	.0098012	.0099886	.0101768	.0103661	.0105562	336
29	.0095663	.0097542	.0099431	.0101328	.0103236	.0105151	348
30	.0095232	.0097129	.0099029	.0100941	.0102861	.0104790	360

Payments to Amortize 1 (Monthly Compounding) (Continued)

Years	12½%	12¾%	13%	13¼%	13½%	13¾%	Months
1	.0890829	.892001	.0893173	.0894347	.0895520	.0896696	12
2	.0473073	.474245	.0475418	.0476594	.0477770	.0478949	24
3	.0334536	.335737	.0336940	.0338145	.0339353	.0340564	36
4	.0265800	.267036	.0268275	.0269518	.0270763	.0272013	48
5	.0224979	.226254	.0227531	.0228813	.0230098	.0231389	60
6	.0198112	.199425	.0200741	.0202063	.0203390	.0204722	72
7	.0179212	.180564	.0181920	.0183282	.0184649	.0186022	84
8	.0165288	.166678	.0168073	.0169475	.0170882	.0172296	96
9	.0154676	.156103	.0157536	.0158977	.0160423	.0161877	108
10	.0146376	.147840	.0149311	.0150789	.0152274	.0153767	120
11	.0139754	.141254	.0142761	.0144277	.0145799	.0147329	132
12	.0134386	.135921	.0137463	.0139014	.0140572	.0142139	144
13	.0129977	.131545	.0133121	.0134706	.0136299	.0137901	156
14	.0126317	.127918	.0129526	.0131145	.0132771	.0134406	168
15	.0123252	.124884	.0126524	.0128174	.0129832	.0131499	180
16	.0120667	.122329	.0123999	.0125679	.0127367	.0129065	192
17	.0118473	.120163	.0121861	.0123570	.0125287	.0127013	204
18	.0116600	.118317	.0120043	.0121779	.0123523	.0125277	216
19	.0114995	.116738	.0118490	.0120251	.0122021	.0123801	228
20	.0113614	.115382	.0117158	.0118944	.0120737	.0122541	240
21	.0112422	.114212	.0116011	.0117820	.0119637	.0121463	252
22	.0111390	.113202	.0115023	.0116853	.0118691	.0120538	264
23	.0110494	.112326	.0114168	.0116018	.0117876	.0119743	276
24	.0109714	.111566	.0113427	.0115296	.0117173	.0119058	288
25	.0109035	.110906	.0112784	.0114671	.0116564	.0118467	300
26	.0108443	.110329	.0112224	.0114128	.0116038	.0117924	312
27	.0107925	.109827	.0111738	.0113656	.0115581	.0117482	324
28	.0107471	.109388	.0111313	.0113246	.0115185	.0117099	336
29	.0107074	.109004	.0110943	.0112889	.0114841	.0116767	348
30	.0106726	.108670	.0110620	.0112578	.0114541	.0116512	360

Payments to Amortize 1 (Monthly Compounding) (Continued)

Years	14%	14¼%	14½%	14¾%	15%	Months
1	.0897871	.0899048	.0900225	.0901404	.0902584	12
2	.0480129	.0481311	.0482494	.0483680	.0484867	24
3	.0341776	.0342992	.0344210	.0345431	.0346654	36
4	.0273265	.0274521	.0275780	.0277042	.0278308	48
5	.0232683	.0233981	.0235283	.0236590	.0237900	60
6	.0206057	.0207399	.0208744	.0210095	.0211451	72
7	.0187400	.0188784	.0190173	.0191568	.0192968	84
8	.0173715	.0175141	.0176573	.0178011	.0179454	96
9	.0163337	.0164804	.0166277	.0167758	.0169243	108
10	.0155266	.0156774	.0158287	.0159808	.0161335	120
11	.0148867	.0150412	.0151964	.0153525	.0155091	132
12	.0143713	.0145295	.0146885	.0148483	.0150088	144
13	.0139510	.0141129	.0142754	.0144388	.0146029	156
14	.0136049	.0137701	.0139360	.0141029	.0142704	168
15	.0133174	.0134858	.0136550	.0138251	.0139959	180
16	.0130770	.0132485	.0134207	.0135938	.0137677	192
17	.0128748	.0130491	.0132242	.0134003	.0135770	204
18	.0127038	.0128809	.0130587	.0132375	.0134169	216
19	.0125588	.0127384	.0129188	.0131000	.0132820	228
20	.0124352	.0126172	.0128000	.0129836	.0131679	240
21	.0123297	.0125139	.0126989	.0128847	.0130712	252
22	.0122393	.0124256	.0126126	.0128004	.0129890	264
23	.0121617	.0123500	.0125389	.0127286	.0129190	276
24	.0120950	.0122851	.0124758	.0126672	.0128593	288
25	.0120376	.0122293	.0124216	.0126147	.0128083	300
26	.0119881	.0121814	.0123751	.0125696	.0127647	312
27	.0119453	.0121400	.0123351	.0125310	.0127274	324
28	.0119084	.0121043	.0123007	.0124978	.0126954	336
29	.0118764	.0120735	.0122711	.0124693	.0126680	348
30	.0118487	.0120469	.0122456	.0124448	.0126444	360

APPENDIX 2 REMAINING BALANCE TABLES

To accurately judge the value of accelerating your mortgage, compare the rate of repayment for various loan terms.

Remaining balance tables report the percentage of the loan that remains unpaid at the end of each year. These tables can be used to calculate the value of different acceleration plans or to estimate the amount of equity you have built up during the loan term. For example, turn to the 10 percent remaining balance table. The columns list percentages of the loan outstanding based on original loan terms at 5-year intervals from 10 to 30 years.

On a 30-year term, you have paid off only half the loan during the 24th year. But the same loan, paid over a 15-year term, is half paid during the 10th year. For the additional payment, acceleration is substantial.

Example. You are paying an $80,000 loan at 10 percent with a 30-year term. What will your balance be at the end of each 5 years?

Solution. Multiply the percentage shown in the 30-year column for 10 percent interest, by the amount of the loan. The answer is the approximate amount still due to the lender at the end of each year:

End of Year	Percentage	Original Loan	Amount Due
5	96.6%	$80,000	$77,280
10	90.9	80,000	72,720
15	81.7	80,000	65,360
20	66.4	80,000	53,120
25	41.3	80,000	33,040
30	0	80,000	0

The following pages include remaining balance tables at ¼ percent intervals between 8 and 15 percent.

Remaining Balance Tables

Age of Loan	8%					8¼%				
	Original Term					Original Term				
	10	15	20	25	30	10	15	20	25	30
1	93.2%	96.4%	97.9%	98.7%	99.2%	93.3%	96.5%	98.0%	98.7%	99.2%
2	85.8	92.5	95.6	97.3	98.3	86.0	92.7	95.7	97.4	98.3
3	77.8	88.3	93.1	95.7	97.3	78.1	88.5	93.3	95.9	97.4
4	69.2	83.7	90.4	94.1	96.2	69.5	84.0	90.7	94.3	96.4
5	59.8	78.8	87.5	92.3	95.1	60.1	79.1	87.3	92.5	95.3
6	49.7	73.4	84.4	90.3	93.8	50.0	73.8	84.7	90.6	94.1
7	38.7	67.6	81.0	88.2	92.5	39.0	68.0	81.4	88.6	92.8
8	26.8	61.3	77.3	85.9	91.0	27.1	61.8	77.7	86.3	91.4
9	14.0	54.5	73.3	83.5	89.4	14.1	55.0	73.8	83.9	89.8
10	0	47.1	68.9	80.8	87.7	0	47.6	69.5	81.3	88.2
11		39.2	64.3	77.9	85.9		40.0	64.8	78.4	86.4
12		30.5	59.2	74.7	83.9		30.9	59.7	75.3	84.4
13		21.1	53.7	71.3	81.7		21.4	54.2	71.9	82.3
14		11.0	47.7	67.6	79.3		11.1	48.3	68.3	80.0
15		0	41.3	63.6	76.8		0	41.8	64.3	77.4
16			34.3	59.3	74.0			34.7	60.0	74.7
17			26.7	54.6	71.0			27.1	55.3	71.8
18			18.5	49.5	67.8			18.8	50.2	68.5
19			9.6	44.0	64.3			9.8	44.7	65.0
20			0	38.1	60.5			0	38.7	61.3
21				31.6	56.4				32.1	57.1
22				24.6	51.9				25.1	52.7
23				17.1	47.1				17.4	47.8
24				8.9	41.9				9.1	42.6
25				0	36.2				0	36.8
26					30.1					30.6
27					23.4					23.9
28					16.2					16.6
29					8.4					8.6
30					0					0

Remaining Balance Tables (Continued)

Age of Loan	8½% Original Term 10	15	20	25	30	8¾% Original Term 10	15	20	25	30
1	93.4%	96.6%	98.0%	98.8%	99.2%	93.5%	96.6%	98.1%	98.8%	99.3%
2	86.2	92.8	95.8	97.5	98.4	86.3	92.9	96.0	97.6	98.5
3	78.3	88.7	93.5	96.0	97.5	78.5	88.9	93.7	96.2	97.6
4	69.7	84.3	90.9	94.5	96.6	70.0	84.5	91.2	94.7	96.7
5	60.4	79.4	88.1	92.8	95.5	60.7	79.8	88.4	93.0	95.7
6	50.3	74.2	85.1	90.9	94.3	50.6	74.5	85.4	91.2	94.6
7	39.3	68.4	81.8	88.9	93.1	39.6	68.8	82.2	89.3	93.4
8	27.3	62.2	78.2	86.7	91.7	27.5	62.6	78.6	87.1	92.0
9	14.2	55.4	74.3	84.4	90.2	14.4	55.8	74.7	84.8	90.6
10	0	48.0	70.0	81.8	88.6	0	48.4	70.5	82.3	89.0
11		40.0	68.4	79.0	86.8		40.4	65.9	79.5	87.3
12		31.2	60.3	75.9	84.9		31.5	60.9	76.5	85.4
13		21.7	54.8	72.5	82.8		21.9	55.4	73.1	83.4
14		11.3	48.8	68.9	80.6		11.4	49.4	69.5	81.2
15		0	42.3	65.0	78.1		0	42.8	65.0	78.7
16			35.2	60.6	75.4			35.7	61.3	76.1
17			27.5	56.0	72.5			27.9	56.6	73.2
18			19.1	50.9	69.3			19.4	51.5	70.0
19			10.0	45.3	65.8			10.1	45.9	66.5
20			0	39.3	62.0			0	39.8	62.8
21				32.7	57.9				33.2	58.7
22				25.5	53.4				26.0	54.2
23				17.7	48.6				18.0	49.3
24				9.2	43.3				9.4	44.0
25				0	37.5				0	38.1
26					31.2					31.8
27					24.4					24.8
28					16.9					17.3
29					8.8					9.0
30					0					0

Remaining Balance Tables (Continued)

Age of Loan	9% Original Term 10	15	20	25	30	9¼% Original Term 10	15	20	25	30
1	93.5%	96.7%	98.1%	98.9%	99.3%	93.6%	96.8%	98.2%	98.9%	99.4%
2	86.5	93.1	96.1	97.7	98.6	86.6	93.2	96.2	97.8	98.6
3	78.7	89.1	93.8	96.3	97.8	79.0	89.3	94.0	96.5	97.9
4	70.3	84.8	91.4	94.9	96.9	70.5	85.1	91.6	95.1	97.0
5	61.0	80.1	88.7	93.3	95.9	61.3	80.4	89.0	93.5	96.1
6	50.9	74.9	85.8	91.5	94.8	51.2	75.3	86.1	91.8	95.0
7	39.8	69.2	82.6	89.6	93.6	40.1	69.6	83.0	89.9	93.9
8	27.7	63.0	79.1	87.5	92.4	28.0	63.5	79.5	87.9	92.7
9	14.5	56.3	75.2	85.2	91.0	14.6	56.7	75.7	85.7	91.3
10	0	48.9	71.0	82.7	89.4	0	49.3	71.5	83.2	89.8
11		40.8	66.4	80.0	87.8		41.2	67.0	80.5	88.2
12		31.9	61.4	77.0	85.9		32.3	62.0	77.6	86.4
13		22.2	55.9	73.7	83.9		22.5	56.5	74.3	84.4
14		11.6	49.9	70.2	81.7		11.8	50.5	70.8	82.3
15		0	43.3	66.3	79.3		0	43.9	66.9	79.9
16			36.2	62.0	76.7			36.6	62.6	77.4
17			28.3	57.3	73.8			28.7	57.9	74.5
18			19.7	52.2	70.7			20.0	52.8	71.4
19			10.3	46.6	67.3			10.5	47.2	68.0
20			0	40.4	63.5			0	41.0	64.3
21				33.7	59.4				34.3	60.2
22				26.4	54.9				26.8	55.7
23				18.4	50.0				18.7	50.7
24				9.6	44.6				9.8	45.3
25				0	38.8				0	39.4
26					32.3					32.9
27					25.3					25.8
28					17.6					18.0
29					9.2					9.4
30					0					0

Remaining Balance Tables (Continued)

Age of Loan	9½% Original Term 10	15	20	25	30	9¾% Original Term 10	15	20	25	30
1	93.7%	96.8%	98.2%	99.0%	99.4%	93.8%	96.9%	98.3%	99.0%	99.4%
2	86.8	93.4	96.3	97.8	98.7	86.9	93.5	96.4	97.9	98.8
3	79.2	89.5	94.2	96.6	98.0	79.4	89.7	94.3	96.7	98.1
4	70.8	85.3	91.8	95.2	97.1	71.1	85.6	92.1	95.4	97.3
5	61.6	80.7	89.3	93.7	96.2	61.9	81.0	89.5	94.0	96.4
6	51.5	75.6	86.4	92.1	95.3	51.8	76.0	86.8	92.4	95.5
7	40.4	70.0	83.3	90.3	94.2	40.7	70.4	83.7	90.6	94.4
8	28.2	63.9	79.9	88.3	93.0	28.4	64.3	80.3	88.6	93.3
9	14.8	57.1	76.2	86.1	91.7	14.9	57.6	76.6	86.5	92.0
10	0	49.7	72.0	83.7	90.2	0	50.2	72.5	84.1	90.6
11		41.6	67.5	81.0	88.6		42.0	68.0	81.5	89.0
12		32.6	62.5	78.1	86.9		33.0	63.1	78.6	87.3
13		22.7	57.0	74.9	85.0		23.0	57.6	75.5	85.5
14		11.9	51.0	71.4	82.8		12.1	51.6	72.0	83.4
15		0	44.4	67.5	80.5		0	44.9	68.2	81.1
16			37.1	63.3	78.0			37.6	63.9	78.6
17			29.1	58.6	75.2			29.5	59.2	75.8
18			20.3	53.5	72.1			20.6	54.1	72.8
19			10.6	47.8	68.0			10.8	48.4	69.4
20			0	41.6	65.0			0	42.2	65.7
21				34.8	60.9				35.3	61.6
22				27.3	56.4				27.7	57.1
23				19.0	51.5				19.4	52.2
24				10.0	46.0				10.2	46.7
25				0	40.0				0	40.7
26					33.5					34.0
27					26.3					26.7
28					18.3					18.7
29					9.6					9.8
30					0					0

Remaining Balance Tables (Continued)

Age of Loan	10%					10¼%				
	Original Term					Original Term				
	10	15	20	25	30	10	15	20	25	30
1	93.9%	97.0%	98.4%	99.1%	99.4%	94.0%	97.0%	98.4%	99.1%	99.5%
2	87.1	93.6	96.5	98.0	98.8	87.2	93.8	96.6	98.1	98.9
3	79.6	89.9	94.5	96.9	98.2	79.8	90.1	94.7	97.0	98.2
4	71.3	85.8	92.3	95.6	97.4	71.6	86.1	92.5	95.7	97.5
5	62.2	81.3	89.8	94.2	96.6	62.5	81.6	90.1	94.4	96.7
6	52.1	76.3	87.1	92.6	95.7	52.4	76.7	87.4	92.9	95.9
7	41.0	70.8	84.1	90.9	94.7	41.2	71.2	84.4	91.2	94.9
8	28.6	64.7	80.8	89.0	93.5	28.9	65.2	81.2	89.3	93.8
9	15.0	58.0	77.1	86.9	92.3	15.2	58.4	77.5	87.3	92.6
10	0	50.6	73.0	84.6	90.9	0	51.0	73.5	85.0	91.3
11		42.4	68.5	82.0	89.4		42.8	69.1	82.5	89.8
12		33.3	63.6	79.2	87.8		33.7	64.1	79.7	88.2
13		23.3	58.1	76.0	85.9		23.6	58.7	76.6	86.4
14		12.2	52.1	72.6	83.9		12.4	52.6	73.2	84.4
15		0	45.4	68.8	81.7		0	45.9	69.4	82.2
16			38.1	64.5	79.2			38.5	65.2	79.8
17			29.9	59.9	76.5			30.3	60.5	77.1
18			20.9	54.7	73.4			21.2	55.4	74.1
19			11.0	49.1	70.1			11.2	49.7	70.8
20			0	42.8	66.4			0	43.4	67.1
21				35.8	62.3				36.4	63.0
22				28.2	57.8				28.6	58.5
23				19.7	52.9				20.0	53.6
24				10.3	47.4				10.5	48.0
25				0	41.3				0	41.9
26					34.6					35.2
27					27.2					27.7
28					19.0					19.4
29					10.0					10.2
30					0					0

Remaining Balance Tables (Continued)

Age of Loan	10½% Original Term 10	15	20	25	30	10¾% Original Term 10	15	20	25	30
1	94.0%	97.1%	98.5%	99.1%	99.5%	94.1%	97.2%	98.5%	99.2%	99.5%
2	87.4	93.9	96.7	98.2	98.9	87.5	94.0	96.8	98.2	99.0
3	80.0	90.3	94.8	97.1	98.3	80.2	90.5	95.0	97.2	98.4
4	71.9	86.3	92.7	95.9	97.6	72.1	86.6	92.9	96.1	97.8
5	62.8	81.9	90.3	94.6	96.9	63.1	82.2	90.6	94.8	97.0
6	52.7	77.0	87.7	93.1	96.0	53.0	77.4	88.0	93.3	96.2
7	41.5	71.6	84.8	91.5	95.1	41.8	72.0	85.1	91.8	95.3
8	29.1	65.6	81.6	89.7	94.1	29.3	66.0	82.0	90.0	94.3
9	15.3	58.9	78.0	87.7	92.9	15.5	59.3	78.4	88.0	93.2
10	0	51.4	74.0	85.4	91.6	0	51.9	74.5	85.8	92.0
11		43.2	69.6	82.9	90.2		43.6	70.1	83.4	90.6
12		34.0	64.7	80.2	88.6		34.4	65.2	80.7	89.0
13		23.8	59.2	77.1	86.9		24.1	59.8	77.7	87.3
14		12.5	53.2	73.7	84.9		12.7	53.7	74.3	85.4
15		0	46.5	70.0	82.8		0	47.0	70.6	83.3
16			39.0	65.8	80.4			39.5	66.4	80.9
17			30.7	61.2	77.7			31.1	61.8	78.3
18			21.5	56.0	74.7			21.8	56.6	75.4
19			11.3	50.3	71.4			11.5	50.9	72.1
20			0	43.9	67.8			0	44.5	68.5
21				36.9	63.7				37.4	64.4
22				29.1	59.2				29.5	59.9
23				20.4	54.3				20.7	54.9
24				10.7	48.7				10.9	49.4
25				0	42.6				0	43.2
26					35.7					36.3
27					28.1					28.6
28					19.7					20.1
29					10.4					10.6
30					0					0

Remaining Balance Tables (Continued)

Age of Loan	11% Original Term 10	15	20	25	30	11¼% Original Term 10	15	20	25	30
1	94.2%	97.2%	98.5%	99.2%	99.6%	94.3%	97.3%	98.6%	99.2%	99.6%
2	87.7	94.1	96.9	98.3	99.1	87.8	94.3	97.0	98.4	99.1
3	80.5	90.7	95.1	97.3	98.5	80.7	90.9	95.2	97.4	98.6
4	72.4	86.8	93.1	96.2	97.9	72.6	87.1	93.3	96.3	98.0
5	63.4	82.5	90.8	95.0	97.2	63.6	82.8	91.1	95.1	97.0
6	53.3	77.7	88.3	93.6	96.4	53.6	78.1	88.6	93.8	96.6
7	42.1	72.4	85.5	92.0	95.5	42.4	72.7	85.8	92.3	95.7
8	29.6	66.4	82.3	90.3	94.6	29.8	66.8	82.7	90.6	94.8
9	15.6	59.7	78.8	88.4	93.5	15.7	60.1	79.3	88.7	93.7
10	0	52.3	74.9	86.2	92.3	0	52.7	75.4	86.6	92.6
11		44.0	70.6	83.8	90.9		44.4	71.1	84.3	91.3
12		34.7	65.7	81.2	89.4		35.1	66.2	81.6	89.8
13		24.4	60.3	78.2	87.7		24.7	60.8	78.7	88.2
14		12.9	54.2	74.9	85.9		13.0	54.8	75.4	86.3
15		0	47.5	71.2	83.8		0	48.0	71.7	84.3
16			39.9	67.0	81.5			40.4	67.6	82.0
17			31.5	62.4	78.9			31.9	63.0	79.4
18			22.2	57.2	76.0			22.5	57.9	76.6
19			11.7	51.5	72.7			11.9	52.1	73.4
20			0	45.1	69.1			0	45.7	69.8
21				37.9	65.1				38.4	65.8
22				29.9	60.6				30.4	61.3
23				21.0	55.6				21.4	56.3
24				11.1	50.0				11.3	50.7
25				0	43.8				0	44.4
26					36.9					37.4
27					29.1					29.6
28					20.4					20.8
29					10.8					11.0
30					0					0

Remaining Balance Tables (Continued)

Age of Loan	11½% Original Term 10	15	20	25	30	11¾% Original Term 10	15	20	25	30
1	94.3%	97.3%	98.6%	99.3%	99.6%	94.4%	97.4%	98.7%	99.3%	99.6%
2	88.0	94.4	97.1	98.4	99.1	88.1	94.5	97.2	98.5	99.2
3	80.9	91.0	95.4	97.5	98.6	81.1	91.2	95.5	97.6	98.7
4	72.9	87.3	93.5	96.5	98.1	73.1	87.5	93.6	96.6	98.2
5	63.9	83.1	91.3	95.3	97.4	64.2	83.4	91.5	95.5	97.6
6	53.9	78.4	88.9	94.0	96.7	54.2	78.7	89.1	94.2	96.9
7	42.6	73.1	86.2	92.6	95.9	42.9	73.5	86.5	92.8	96.1
8	30.0	67.2	83.1	90.9	95.0	30.3	67.6	83.5	91.2	95.2
9	15.9	60.6	79.7	89.1	94.0	16.0	61.0	80.1	89.4	94.2
10	0	53.1	75.9	87.0	92.9	0	53.5	76.3	87.4	93.1
11		44.8	71.6	84.7	91.6		45.2	72.0	85.1	91.9
12		35.4	66.7	82.1	90.2		35.8	67.3	82.6	90.5
13		24.9	61.3	79.2	88.6		25.2	61.9	79.7	89.0
14		13.2	55.3	76.0	86.8		13.4	55.8	76.5	87.2
15		0	48.5	72.3	84.8		0	49.0	72.9	85.2
16			40.9	68.2	82.5			41.4	68.8	83.0
17			32.3	63.6	80.0			32.8	64.2	80.5
18			22.8	58.5	77.2			23.1	59.1	77.8
19			12.0	52.7	74.0			12.2	53.3	74.6
20			0	46.2	70.4			0	46.8	71.1
21				39.0	66.5				39.5	67.1
22				30.8	62.0				31.3	62.6
23				21.7	57.0				22.0	57.6
24				11.5	51.3				11.7	52.0
25				0	45.0				0	45.6
26					38.0					38.5
27					30.0					30.5
28					21.1					21.5
29					11.2					11.4
30					0					0

Remaining Balance Tables (Continued)

Age of Loan	12% Original Term 10	15	20	25	30	12¼% Original Term 10	15	20	25	30
1	94.5%	97.5%	98.7%	99.3%	99.6%	94.6%	97.5%	98.8%	99.4%	99.7%
2	88.3	94.6	97.3	98.6	99.2	88.4	94.7	97.4	98.6	99.3
3	81.3	91.4	95.7	97.7	98.8	81.5	91.6	95.8	97.8	98.8
4	73.4	87.8	93.8	96.7	98.3	73.6	88.0	94.0	96.9	98.3
5	64.5	83.7	91.7	95.7	97.7	64.8	83.9	92.0	95.8	97.8
6	54.5	79.0	89.4	94.4	97.0	54.8	79.4	89.7	94.6	97.1
7	43.2	73.8	86.8	93.1	98.3	43.5	74.2	87.1	93.3	96.4
8	30.5	68.0	83.8	91.5	95.4	30.7	68.4	84.2	91.8	95.6
9	16.2	61.4	80.5	89.7	99.5	16.3	61.8	80.9	90.1	94.7
10	0	54.0	76.8	87.8	93.4	0	54.4	77.2	88.1	93.7
11		45.6	72.5	85.5	92.2		46.0	73.0	85.9	92.5
12		36.1	67.8	83.0	90.9		36.5	68.2	83.5	91.2
13		25.5	62.4	80.2	89.4		25.8	62.9	80.7	89.7
14		13.5	56.3	77.0	87.6		13.7	56.8	77.5	88.1
15		0	49.5	73.4	85.7		0	50.0	74.0	86.2
16			41.8	69.4	83.6			42.3	69.9	84.0
17			33.2	64.8	81.1			33.6	65.4	81.6
18			23.4	59.7	78.3			23.7	60.3	78.9
19			12.4	53.9	75.2			12.6	54.5	75.8
20			0	47.4	71.7			0	47.9	72.3
21				40.0	67.7				40.5	68.4
22				31.7	63.3				32.2	63.9
23				22.4	58.3				22.7	58.9
24				11.9	52.6				12.1	53.3
25				0	46.2				0	46.8
26					39.1					39.6
27					31.0					31.4
28					21.9					22.2
29					11.6					11.8
30					0					0

Remaining Balance Tables (Continued)

Age of Loan	12½%					12¾%				
	Original Term					Original Term				
	10	15	20	25	30	10	15	20	25	30
1	94.6%	97.6%	98.8%	99.4%	99.7%	94.7%	97.6%	98.8%	99.4%	99.7%
2	88.6	94.8	97.4	98.7	99.3	88.7	94.9	97.5	98.7	99.3
3	81.7	91.7	95.9	97.9	98.9	81.9	91.9	96.0	98.0	99.0
4	73.9	88.2	94.2	97.0	98.4	74.1	88.4	94.3	97.1	98.5
5	65.1	84.2	92.2	96.0	97.9	65.3	84.5	92.4	96.1	98.0
6	55.1	79.7	89.9	94.8	97.3	55.4	80.0	90.2	95.0	97.4
7	43.8	74.6	87.4	93.5	96.6	44.0	74.9	87.7	93.7	96.7
8	30.9	68.8	84.5	92.0	95.8	31.2	69.2	84.9	92.3	96.0
9	16.4	62.2	81.3	90.4	94.9	16.6	62.6	81.7	90.7	95.2
10	0	54.8	77.6	88.5	93.9	0	55.2	78.0	88.8	94.2
11		46.4	73.5	86.3	92.8		46.8	73.9	86.7	93.1
12		36.8	68.7	83.9	91.5		37.2	69.2	84.3	91.9
13		26.1	63.4	81.1	90.1		26.3	63.9	81.6	90.4
14		13.8	57.4	78.0	88.5		14.0	57.9	78.5	88.8
15		0	50.5	74.5	86.6		0	51.0	75.0	87.0
16			42.7	70.5	84.5			43.2	71.1	85.0
17			34.0	66.0	82.1			34.4	66.5	82.6
18			24.0	60.8	79.4			24.3	61.4	80.0
19			12.8	55.0	76.4			12.9	55.6	76.9
20			0	48.5	72.9			0	49.0	73.5
21				41.0	69.0				41.5	69.6
22				32.6	64.6				33.0	65.2
23				23.1	59.6				23.4	60.2
24				12.2	53.9				12.4	54.5
25				0	47.4				0	48.0
26					40.2					40.7
27					31.9					32.4
28					22.6					22.9
29					12.0					12.2
30					0					0

Remaining Balance Tables (Continued)

Age of Loan	13% Original Term 10	15	20	25	30	13¼% Original Term 10	15	20	25	30
1	94.8%	97.7%	98.9%	99.4%	99.7%	94.9%	97.7%	98.9%	99.5%	99.7%
2	88.8	95.0	97.0	98.8	99.4	89.0	95.2	97.7	98.8	99.4
3	82.1	92.0	96.1	98.1	99.0	82.3	92.2	96.3	98.1	99.1
4	74.4	88.6	94.5	97.2	98.6	74.6	88.8	94.6	97.3	98.6
5	65.6	84.7	92.6	96.3	98.1	65.9	85.0	92.8	96.4	98.2
6	55.7	80.3	90.5	95.2	97.5	56.0	80.6	90.7	95.4	97.6
7	44.3	75.3	88.0	94.0	96.9	44.6	75.6	88.3	94.2	97.0
8	31.4	69.6	85.2	92.6	96.2	31.6	69.9	85.6	92.8	96.3
9	16.7	63.0	82.1	91.0	95.4	16.9	63.4	82.4	91.2	95.6
10	0	55.6	78.5	89.1	94.4	0	56.0	78.9	89.5	94.7
11		47.2	74.4	87.1	93.4		47.6	74.8	87.4	93.6
12		37.6	69.7	84.7	92.2		37.9	70.2	85.1	92.4
13		26.6	64.4	82.1	90.8		26.9	64.9	82.5	91.1
14		14.2	58.4	79.0	89.2		14.3	58.9	79.5	89.6
15		0	51.5	75.5	87.4		0	52.0	76.1	87.8
16			43.7	71.6	85.4			44.1	72.1	85.8
17			34.8	67.1	83.1			35.2	67.7	83.6
18			24.6	62.0	80.5			25.0	62.6	81.0
19			13.1	56.2	77.5			13.3	56.8	78.0
20			0	49.6	74.1			0	50.1	74.7
21				42.0	70.2				42.6	70.8
22				33.5	65.8				33.9	66.4
23				23.7	60.8				24.1	61.4
24				12.6	55.1				12.8	55.7
25				0	48.6				0	49.2
26					41.2					41.8
27					32.8					33.3
28					23.3					23.6
29					12.4					12.6
30					0					0

Remaining Balance Tables (Continued)

Age of Loan	13½% Original Term 10	15	20	25	30	13¾% Original Term 10	15	20	25	30
1	94.9%	97.8%	99.0%	99.5%	99.7%	95.0%	97.8%	99.0%	99.5%	99.8%
2	89.1	95.3	97.7	98.9	99.4	89.3	95.4	97.8	98.9	99.5
3	82.5	92.4	96.4	98.2	99.1	82.7	92.5	96.5	98.3	99.2
4	74.9	89.1	94.8	97.4	98.7	75.1	89.3	95.0	97.5	98.8
5	66.2	85.3	93.0	96.5	98.3	66.5	85.5	93.2	96.7	98.4
6	56.2	80.9	90.9	95.5	97.8	56.5	81.2	91.2	95.7	97.9
7	44.9	76.0	88.6	94.4	97.2	45.2	76.3	88.9	94.6	97.3
8	31.9	70.3	85.9	93.0	96.5	32.1	70.7	86.2	93.3	96.7
9	17.0	63.8	82.8	91.5	95.7	17.2	64.2	83.2	91.8	95.9
10	0	56.4	79.3	89.8	94.9	0	56.8	79.7	90.1	95.1
11		48.0	75.3	87.8	93.9		48.3	75.7	88.1	94.1
12		38.3	70.7	85.5	92.7		38.6	71.1	85.9	93.0
13		27.2	65.4	82.9	91.4		27.5	65.9	83.4	91.7
14		14.5	59.4	80.0	89.9		14.7	59.9	80.4	90.3
15		0	52.5	76.6	88.2		0	53.0	77.0	88.6
16			44.6	72.7	86.3			45.1	73.2	86.7
17			35.6	68.2	84.0			36.0	68.8	84.5
18			25.3	63.1	81.5			25.6	63.7	82.0
19			12.5	57.3	78.6			13.7	57.9	79.1
20			0	50.7	75.2			0	51.2	75.8
21				43.1	71.4				43.6	72.0
22				34.4	67.0				34.8	67.6
23				24.4	62.0				24.7	62.6
24				13.0	56.3				13.2	56.9
25				0	49.8				0	50.4
26					42.3					42.8
27					33.8					34.2
28					24.0					24.3
29					12.8					13.0
30					0					0

Remaining Balance Tables (Continued)

Age of Loan	14%					14¼%				
	Original Term					Original Term				
	10	15	20	25	30	10	15	20	25	30
1	95.1%	97.9%	99.0%	99.5%	99.8%	95.1%	97.9%	99.1%	99.6%	99.8%
2	89.4	95.5	97.9	99.0	99.5	89.5	95.6	98.0	99.0	99.5
3	82.9	92.7	96.6	98.4	99.2	83.0	92.8	96.7	98.4	99.2
4	75.4	89.5	95.1	97.6	98.8	75.6	89.7	95.2	97.7	98.9
5	66.7	85.8	93.4	96.8	98.4	67.0	86.0	93.6	96.9	98.5
6	56.8	81.5	91.4	95.9	98.0	57.1	81.8	91.6	96.0	98.1
7	45.4	76.7	89.1	94.7	97.4	45.7	77.0	89.4	94.9	97.6
8	32.3	71.1	86.5	93.5	96.8	32.6	71.4	86.8	93.7	97.0
9	17.3	64.6	83.5	92.1	96.1	17.4	65.0	83.9	92.3	96.3
10	0	57.2	80.1	90.4	95.3	0	57.6	80.5	90.7	95.5
11		48.7	76.1	88.5	94.4		49.1	76.6	88.8	94.6
12		39.0	71.6	86.3	93.3		39.3	72.0	86.7	93.5
13		27.7	66.4	83.8	92.0		28.0	66.8	84.2	92.3
14		14.8	60.4	80.9	90.6		15.0	60.8	81.3	90.9
15		0	53.4	77.5	89.0		0	53.9	78.0	89.3
16			45.5	73.7	87.1			46.0	74.2	87.5
17			36.4	69.3	84.9			36.8	69.8	85.4
18			25.9	64.2	82.5			26.2	64.8	82.9
19			13.9	58.4	79.6			14.0	59.0	80.1
20			0	51.7	76.3			0	52.3	76.8
21				44.1	72.5				44.6	73.1
22				35.2	68.2				35.7	68.8
23				25.1	63.2				25.4	63.8
24				13.4	57.5				13.6	58.1
25				0	50.9				0	51.5
26					43.4					43.9
27					34.7					35.1
28					24.7					25.0
29					13.2					13.4
30					0					0

Remaining Balance Tables (Continued)

Age of Loan	14½% Original Term 10	15	20	25	30	14¾% Original Term 10	15	20	25	30
1	95.2%	98.0%	99.1%	99.6%	99.8%	95.3%	98.0%	99.1%	99.6%	99.8%
2	89.6	95.7	98.0	99.1	99.6	89.8	95.8	98.1	99.1	99.6
3	83.2	93.0	96.8	98.5	99.3	83.4	93.1	96.9	98.6	99.3
4	75.8	89.9	95.4	97.8	99.0	76.1	90.1	95.5	97.9	99.0
5	67.3	86.3	93.7	97.0	98.6	67.6	86.5	93.9	97.2	98.7
6	57.4	82.1	91.9	96.2	98.2	57.7	82.4	92.1	96.3	98.2
7	46.0	77.3	89.7	95.1	97.7	46.3	77.7	89.9	95.3	97.8
8	32.8	71.8	87.1	93.9	97.1	33.0	72.2	87.4	94.1	97.2
9	17.6	65.4	84.2	92.6	96.4	17.7	65.8	84.6	92.8	96.6
10	0	58.0	80.9	91.0	95.7	0	58.4	81.2	91.2	95.9
11		49.5	77.0	89.1	94.8		49.9	77.4	89.5	95.0
12		39.7	72.5	87.0	93.8		40.0	72.9	87.4	94.0
13		28.3	67.3	84.6	92.6		28.6	67.8	85.0	92.9
14		15.2	61.3	81.7	91.2		15.3	61.8	82.2	91.6
15		0	54.4	78.5	89.7		0	54.9	78.9	90.0
16			46.4	74.7	87.9			46.9	75.2	88.2
17			37.2	70.4	85.8			37.6	70.9	86.2
18			26.5	65.3	83.4			26.8	65.9	83.8
19			14.2	59.5	80.6			14.4	60.0	81.1
20			0	52.8	77.4			0	53.3	77.9
21				45.0	73.7				45.5	74.2
22				36.1	69.4				36.5	69.9
23				25.7	64.4				26.1	65.0
24				13.8	58.7				14.0	59.2
25				0	52.1				0	52.6
26					44.4					44.9
27					35.6					36.0
28					25.4					25.7
29					13.6					13.8
30					0					0

Remaining Balance Tables (Continued)

Age of Loan	15% Original Term 10	15	20	25	30
1	95.3%	98.1%	99.1%	99.6%	99.8%
2	89.9	95.8	98.1	99.1	99.6
3	83.6	93.3	97.0	98.6	99.4
4	76.3	90.2	95.6	98.0	99.1
5	67.8	86.8	94.1	97.3	98.7
6	58.0	82.7	92.3	96.4	98.3
7	46.5	78.0	90.2	95.5	97.9
8	33.3	72.5	87.7	94.3	97.4
9	17.9	66.2	84.9	93.0	96.7
10	0	58.8	81.6	91.5	96.0
11		50.3	77.8	89.8	95.2
12		40.4	73.4	87.7	94.2
13		28.9	68.2	85.3	93.1
14		15.5	62.3	82.6	91.8
15		0	53.4	79.4	90.3
16			47.3	75.7	88.6
17			38.0	71.4	86.6
18			27.2	66.4	84.3
19			14.6	60.6	81.5
20			0	53.8	78.4
21				46.0	74.7
22				37.0	70.5
23				26.4	65.5
24				14.2	59.8
25				0	53.2
26					45.4
27					36.5
28					26.1
29					14.0
30					0

APPENDIX 3 SAMPLE ACCELERATION PLANS

To judge the relative savings from various plans of mortgage acceleration, a detailed comparison is the most revealing form of information. In this appendix, the outcome of several plans are presented, including

Yearly summaries of total payments, amounts paid to principal and interest, and ending balances
After-tax interest costs, based on an assumed tax rate of 28 percent
Cash payment comparisons between each plan
Remaining balances for each plan

The appendix is divided into three main sections. First is a comparison between 30-year amortization and a number of fixed payment acceleration plans. Second is a comparison of acceleration by way of different graduating payment methods. And third is a summary of acceleration plans for variable-rate mortgages.

LEVEL-PAYMENT PLANS

The acceleration methods in this section call for payment of the same amount per month or per year. Included in the following tables are samples of repayment for a 10 percent loan with an original balance of $80,000:

1. *Full Amortization, 30 Years.* This plan is a summary of payments, principal, interest, and ending balance without any form of acceleration.

1. Full Amortization, 30 Years

Year	Total Payments	Paid to Interest	Paid to Principal	Balance
				$80,000.00
1	$ 8,424.72	$ 7,979.97	$ 444.75	79,555.25
2	8,424.72	7,933.40	491.32	79,063.93
3	8,424.72	7,881.98	542.74	78,521.19
4	8,424.72	7,825.12	599.60	77,921.59
5	8,424.72	7,762.36	662.36	77,259.23
6	8,424.72	7,692.98	731.74	76,527.49
7	8,424.72	7,616.35	808.37	75,719.12
8	8,424.72	7,531.69	893.03	74,826.09
9	8,424.72	7,438.20	986.52	73,839.57
10	8,424.72	7,334.91	1,089.81	72,749.76
11	8,424.72	7,220.79	1,203.93	71,545.83
12	8,424.72	7.094.72	1,330.00	70,215.83
13	8,424.72	6,955.46	1,469.26	68,746.57
14	8,424.72	6,801.60	1,623.12	67,123.45
15	8,424.72	6,631.64	1,793.08	65,330.37
16	8,424.72	6,443.88	1,980.84	63,349.53
17	8,424.72	6,236.45	2,188.27	61,161.26
18	8,424.72	6,007.33	2,417.39	58,743.87
19	8,424.72	5,754.18	2,670.54	56,073.33
20	8,424.72	5,474.54	2,950.18	53,123.15
21	8,424.72	5,165.61	3,259.11	49,864.04
22	8,424.72	4,824.36	3,600.36	46,263.68
23	8,424.72	4,447.34	3,977.38	42,286.30
24	8,424.72	4,030.85	4,393.87	37,892.43
25	8,424.72	3,570.77	4,853.95	33,038.48
26	8,424.72	3,062.50	5,362.22	27,676.26
27	8,424.72	2,501.02	5,923.70	21,752.56
28	8,424.72	1,880.70	6,544.02	15,208.54
29	8,424.72	1,195.48	7,229.24	7,979.30
30	8,417.78	438.48	7,979.30	0
Total	$252,734.66	$172,734.66	$80,000.00	

2. 15-Year Amortization. This plan shows the outcome for amortization on a 15-year schedule.

3. Increase Payment by $100 per Month. This amortization plan shows how a loan scheduled for 30-year amortization will be paid off when the required monthly payment is increased by $100.

4. Increase Payment by $200 per Month. This variation of level payment calls for an increase above the required 30-year amortization payment of $200 every month.

5. Add $1,000 to Principal Each Year. Under this plan, the monthly payment of $702.06 is made for months 2 through 11. However, on the first month of each year, an additional $1,000 is added to principal.

6. Add $2,000 to Principal Each Year. This plan is identical to plan 5 except that $2,000 is added to the first payment each year.

2. 15-Year Amortization

Year	Total Payments	Paid to Interest	Paid to Principal	Balance
				$80,000.00
1	$ 10,316.28	$ 7,890.84	$ 2,425.44	77,574.56
2	10,316.28	7,636.86	2,679.42	74,895.14
3	10,316.28	7,356.30	2,959.98	71,935.16
4	10,316.28	7,046.33	3,269.95	68,665.21
5	10,316.28	6,703.93	3,612.35	65,052.86
6	10,316.28	6,325.67	3,990.61	61,062.25
7	10,316.28	5,907.80	4,408.48	56,653.77
8	10,316.28	5,446.16	4,870.12	51,783.65
9	10,316.28	4,936.21	5,380.07	46,403.58
10	10,316.28	4,372.86	5,943.42	40,460.16
11	10,316.28	3,750.48	6,565.80	33,894.36
12	10,316.28	3,062.97	7,253.31	26,641.05
13	10,316.28	2,303.46	8,012.82	18,628.23
14	10,316.28	1,464.42	8,851.86	9,776.37
15	10,316.06	539.69	9,776.37	0
Total	$154,743.98	$74,743.98	$80,000.00	

3. Increase Payment by $100 per Month

Year	Total Payments	Paid to Interest	Paid to Principal	Balance
				$80,000.00
1	$ 9,624.72	$ 7,923.42	$ 1,701.30	78,298.70
2	9,624.72	7,745.27	1,879.45	76,419.25
3	9,624.72	7,548.46	2,076.26	74,342.99
4	9,624.72	7,331.05	2,293.67	72,049.32
5	9,624.72	7,090.89	2,533.83	69,515.49
6	9,624.72	6,825.56	2,799.16	66,716.33
7	9,624.72	6,532.47	3,092.25	63,624.08
8	9,624.72	6,208.66	3,416.06	60,208.02
9	9,624.72	5,850.95	3,773.77	56,434.25
10	9,624.72	5,455.79	4,168.93	52,265.32
11	9,624.72	5,019.23	4,605.49	47,659.83
12	9,624.72	4,536.99	5,087.73	42,572.10
13	9,624.72	4,004.22	5,620.50	36,951.60
14	9,624.72	3,415.69	6,209.03	30,742.57
15	9,624.72	2,765.53	6,859.19	23,883.38
16	9,624.72	2,047.28	7,577.44	16,305.94
17	9,624.72	1,253.82	8,370.90	7,935.04
18	8,316.55	381.51	7,935.04	0
Total	$171,936.79	$91,936.79	$80,000.00	

4. Increase Payment by $200 per Month

Year	Total Payments	Paid to Interest	Paid to Principal	Balance
				$80,000.00
1	$ 10,824.72	$ 7,866.88	$ 2,957.84	77,042.16
2	10,824.72	7,557.14	3,267.58	73,774.58
3	10,824.72	7,214.99	3,609.73	70,164.85
4	10,824.72	6,837.02	3,987.70	66,177.15
5	10,824.72	6,419.44	4,405.28	61,771.87
6	10,824.72	5,958.14	4,866.58	56,905.29
7	10,824.72	5,448.56	5,376.16	51,529.13
8	10,824.72	4,885.59	5,939.13	45,590.00
9	10,824.72	4,263.70	6,561.02	39,028.98
10	10,824.72	3,576.66	7,248.06	31,780.92

4. Increase Payment by $200 per Month (Continued)

Year	Total Payments	Paid to Interest	Paid to Principal	Balance
11	$ 10,824.72	$ 2,817.70	$ 8,007.02	$ 23,773.90
12	10,824.72	1,979.26	8,845.46	14,928.44
13	10,824.72	1,053.02	9,771.70	5,156.74
14	5,306.00	149.26	5,156.74	0
Total	$146,027.36	$66,027.36	$80,000.00	

5. Add $1,000 to Principal Each Year

Year	Total Payments	Paid to Interest	Paid to Principal	Balance
				$80,000.00
1	$ 9,424.72	$ 7,884.40	$ 1,540.32	78,459.68
2	9,424.72	7,723.11	1,701.61	76,758.07
3	9,424.72	7,544.92	1,879.80	74,878.27
4	9,424.72	7,348.09	2,076.63	72,801.64
5	9,424.72	7,130.93	2,294.09	70,507.55
6	9,424.72	6,890.41	2,534.31	67,973.24
7	9,424.72	6,625.02	2,799.70	65,173.54
8	9,424.72	6,331.86	3,092.86	62,080.68
9	9,424.72	6,008.02	3,416.70	58,663.98
10	9,424.72	5,550.26	3,774.46	54,889.52
11	9,424.72	5,255.00	4,169.72	50,719.80
12	9,424.72	4,818.38	4,606.34	46,113.46
13	9,424.72	4,336.04	5,088.68	41,024.78
14	9,424.72	3,803.19	5,621.53	35,403.25
15	9,424.72	3,214.55	6,210.17	29,193.08
16	9,424.72	2,564.26	6,860.46	22,332.62
17	9,424.72	1,845.89	7,578.83	12,753.79
18	9,424.72	1,052.27	8,372.45	6,381.34
19	6,593.00	211.66	6,381.34	0
Total	$176,237.96	$96,237.96	$80,000.00	

6. Add $2,000 to Principal Each Year

Year	Total Payments	Paid to Interest	Paid to Principal	Balance
				$80,000.00
1	$ 10,424.72	$ 7,788.84	$ 2,635.88	77,364.12
2	10,424.72	7,512.81	2,911.91	74,452.21
3	10,424.72	7,207.89	3,216.83	71,235.38
4	10,424.72	6,871.07	3,553.65	67,681.73
5	10,424.72	6,498.93	3,925.79	63,755.94
6	10,424.72	6,087.86	4,336.86	59,419.08
7	10,424.72	5,633.72	4,791.00	54,628.08
8	10,424.72	5,132.05	5,292.67	49,335.41
9	10,424.72	4,577.83	5,846.89	43,488.52
10	10,424.72	3,965.58	6,459.14	37,029.38
11	10,424.72	3,289,23	7,135.49	29,893.89
12	10,424.72	2,542.05	7,882.67	22,011.22
13	10,424.72	1,716.65	8,708.07	13,303.15
14	10,424.72	804.77	9,619.95	3,683.20
15	3,724.97	41.77	3,683.20	0
Total	$149,671.05	$69,671.05	$80,000.00	

After-Tax Interest Cost

The five schedules that follow break down the interest costs for each form of level-payment acceleration and compare those costs to full amortization.

This comparison is made on an after-tax basis, assuming a federal tax rate of 28 percent. Thus, every dollar of interest paid will reduce your tax liability by $0.28. The purpose of comparing on an after-tax basis is to evaluate the benefits of acceleration net of the advantage of claiming itemized deductions.

Each schedule shows the full amortization interest paid, less a 28 percent tax advantage, and the net, which is compared to each plan's gross, tax deduction, and net. The difference is shown in the last column.

Cash Payments

The following table (pp. 203–207) shows how each level-payment acceleration plan works out in terms of the total amount paid to a lender.

A comparison of total interest costs over the term of your mortgage reveals the potential savings and reduction in the total cost of your home.

Remaining Balances

In Appendix 2, the remaining balances for various interest rates and repayment terms were summarized. In the table on pages 208–209, a summary and comparison of each level-payment plan are shown.

The rate of amortization is determined by the number of years in the full term, and the rate of acceleration is applied against the full mortgage debt. This comparison shows the relative advantages of each level-payment plan.

After-Tax Interest Cost: 15-Year Amortization

	Full Amortization			With Acceleration			
Year	Interest	Tax Savings	After-Tax Cost	Interest	Tax Savings	After-Tax Cost	Net Saved
1	$ 7,980	$ 2,234	$ 5,746	$ 7,891	$ 2,209	$ 5,682	$ 64
2	7,933	2,221	5,712	7,637	2,138	5,499	213
3	7,882	2,207	5,675	7,356	2,060	5,296	379
4	7,825	2,191	5,634	7,046	1,973	5,073	561
5	7,762	2,173	5,589	6,704	1,877	4,827	762
6	7,693	2,154	5,539	6,326	1,771	4,555	984
7	7,616	2,132	5,484	5,908	1,654	4,254	1,230
8	7,532	2,109	5,423	5,446	1,525	3,921	1,502
9	7,438	2,083	5,355	4,936	1,382	3,554	1,801
10	7,335	2,054	5,281	4,373	1,224	3,149	2,132
11	7,221	2,022	5,199	3,750	1,050	2,700	2,499
12	7,095	1,987	5,108	3,063	858	2,205	2,903
13	6,955	1,947	5,008	2,303	645	1,658	3,350
14	6,802	1,905	4,897	1,464	410	1,054	3,843
15	6,632	1,857	4,775	540	151	389	4,386
16	6,444	1,804	4,640				4,640
17	6,236	1,746	4,490				4,490
18	6,007	1,682	4,325				4,325
19	5,754	1,611	4,143				4,143
20	5,475	1,533	3,942				3,942
21	5,166	1,446	3,720				3,720
22	4,824	1,351	3,473				3,473
23	4,447	1,245	3,202				3,202
24	4,031	1,129	2,902				2,902
25	3,571	1,000	2,571				2,571
26	3,063	858	2,205				2,205
27	2,501	700	1,801				1,801
28	1,881	527	1,354				1,354
29	1,195	335	860				860
30	438	123	315				315
Total	$172,734	$48,366	$124,368	$74,743	$20,927	$53,816	$70,552

After-Tax Interest Cost: Increase Payment by $100 Per Month

	Full Amortization			With Acceleration			
Year	Interest	Tax Savings	After-Tax Cost	Interest	Tax Savings	After-Tax Cost	Net Saved
1	$ 7,980	$ 2,234	$ 5,746	$ 7,923	$ 2,218	$ 5,705	$ 41
2	7,933	2,221	5,712	7,745	2,169	5,576	136
3	7,882	2,207	5,675	7,548	2,113	5,435	240
4	7,825	2,191	5,634	7,331	2,053	5,278	356
5	7,762	2,173	5,589	7,091	1,985	5,106	483
6	7,693	2,154	5,539	6,825	1,911	4,914	625
7	7,616	2,132	5,484	6,532	1,829	4,703	781
8	7,532	2,109	5,423	6,209	1,739	4,470	953
9	7,438	2,083	5,355	5,851	1,638	4,213	1,142
10	7,335	2,054	5,281	5,456	1,528	3,928	1,353
11	7,221	2,022	5,199	5,019	1,405	3,614	1,585
12	7,095	1,987	5,108	4,537	1,270	3,267	1,841
13	6,955	1,947	5,008	4,004	1,121	2,883	2,125
14	6,802	1,905	4,897	3,416	956	2,460	2,437
15	6,632	1,857	4,775	2,766	774	1,992	2,783
16	6,444	1,804	4,640	2,047	573	1,474	3,166
17	6,236	1,746	4,490	1,254	351	903	3,587
18	6,007	1,682	4,325	382	107	275	4,050
19	5,754	1,611	4,143				4,143
20	5,475	1,533	3,942				3,942
21	5,166	1,446	3,720				3,720
22	4,824	1,351	3,473				3,473
23	4,447	1,245	3,202				3,202
24	4,031	1,129	2,902				2,902
25	3,571	1,000	2,571				2,571
26	3,063	858	2,205				2,205
27	2,501	700	1,801				1,801
28	1,881	527	1,354				1,354
29	1,195	335	860				860
30	438	123	315				315
Total	$172,734	$48,366	$124,368	$91,936	$25,740	$66,196	$58,172

After-Tax Interest Cost: Increase Payment by $200 Per Month

	Full Amortization			With Acceleration			
Year	Interest	Tax Savings	After-Tax Cost	Interest	Tax Savings	After-Tax Cost	Net Saved
1	$ 7,980	$ 2,234	$ 5,746	$ 7,867	$ 2,203	$ 5,664	$ 82
2	7,933	2,221	5,712	7,557	2,116	5,441	271
3	7,882	2,207	5,675	7,215	2,020	5,195	480
4	7,825	2,191	5,634	6,837	1,914	4,923	711
5	7,762	2,173	5,589	6,419	1,797	4,622	967
6	7,693	2,154	5,539	5,958	1,668	4,290	1,249
7	7,616	2,132	5,484	5,449	1,526	3,923	1,561
8	7,532	2,109	5,423	4,886	1,368	3,518	1,905
9	7,438	2,083	5,355	4,264	1,194	3,070	2,285
10	7,335	2,054	5,281	3,577	1,002	2,575	2,706
11	7,221	2,022	5,199	2,818	789	2,029	3,170
12	7,095	1,987	5,108	1,979	554	1,425	3,683
13	6,955	1,947	5,008	1,053	295	758	4,250
14	6,802	1,905	4,897	149	42	107	4,790
15	6,632	1,857	4,775				4,775
16	6,444	1,804	4,640				4,640
17	6,236	1,746	4,490				4,490
18	6,007	1,682	4,325				4,325
19	5,754	1,611	4,143				4,143
20	5,475	1,533	3,942				3,942
21	5,166	1,446	3,720				3,720
22	4,824	1,351	3,473				3,473
23	4,447	1,245	3,202				3,202
24	4,031	1,129	2,902				2,902
25	3,571	1,000	2,571				2,571
26	3,063	858	2,205				2,205
27	2,501	700	1,801				1,801
28	1,881	527	1,354				1,354
29	1,195	335	860				860
30	438	123	315				315
Total	$172,734	$48,366	$124,368	$66,028	$18,488	$47,540	$76,828

After-Tax Interest Cost: Add $1,000 to Principal Each Year

	Full Amortization			With Acceleration			
Year	Interest	Tax Savings	After-Tax Cost	Interest	Tax Savings	After-Tax Cost	Net Saved
1	$ 7,980	$ 2,234	$ 5,746	$ 7,884	$ 2,208	$ 5,676	$ 70
2	7,933	2,221	5,712	7,723	2,162	5,561	151
3	7,882	2,207	5,675	7,545	2,113	5,432	243
4	7,825	2,191	5,634	7,348	2,057	5,291	343
5	7,762	2,173	5,589	7,131	1,997	5,134	455
6	7,693	2,154	5,539	6,890	1,929	4,961	578
7	7,616	2,132	5,484	6,625	1,855	4,770	714
8	7,532	2,109	5,423	6,332	1,773	4,559	864
9	7,438	2,083	5,355	6,008	1,682	4,326	1,029
10	7,335	2,054	5,281	5,650	1,582	4,068	1,213
11	7,221	2,022	5,199	5,255	1,471	3,784	1,415
12	7,095	1,987	5,108	4,818	1,349	3,469	1,639
13	6,955	1,947	5,008	4,336	1,214	3,122	1,886
14	6,802	1,905	4,897	3,803	1,065	2,738	2,159
15	6,632	1,857	4,775	3,215	900	2,315	2,460
16	6,444	1,804	4,640	2,564	718	1,846	2,794
17	6,236	1,746	4,490	1,846	517	1,329	3,161
18	6,007	1,682	4,325	1,052	295	757	3,568
19	5,754	1,611	4,143	212	59	153	3,990
20	5,475	1,533	3,942				3,942
21	5,166	1,446	3,720				3,720
22	4,824	1,351	3,473				3,473
23	4,447	1,245	3,202				3,202
24	4,031	1,129	2,902				2,902
25	3,571	1,000	2,571				2,571
26	3,063	858	2,205				2,205
27	2,501	700	1,801				1,801
28	1,881	527	1,354				1,354
29	1,195	335	860				860
30	438	123	315				315
Total	$172,734	$48,366	$124,368	$96,237	$26,946	$69,291	$55,077

After-Tax Interest Cost: Add $2,000 to Principal Each Year

	Full Amortization			With Acceleration			
Year	Interest	Tax Savings	After-Tax Cost	Interest	Tax Savings	After-Tax Cost	Net Saved
1	$ 7,980	$ 2,234	$ 5,746	$ 7,789	$ 2,181	$ 5,608	$ 138
2	7,933	2,221	5,712	7,513	2,104	5,409	303
3	7,882	2,207	5,675	7,208	2,018	5,190	485
4	7,825	2,191	5,634	6,871	1,924	4,947	687
5	7,762	2,173	5,589	6,499	1,820	4,679	910
6	7,693	2,154	5,539	6,088	1,705	4,383	1,156
7	7,616	2,132	5,484	5,634	1,578	4,056	1,428
8	7,532	2,109	5,423	5,132	1,437	3,695	1,728
9	7,438	2,083	5,355	4,578	1,282	3,296	2,059
10	7,335	2,054	5,281	3,965	1,110	2,855	2,426
11	7,221	2,022	5,199	3,289	921	2,368	2,831
12	7,095	1,987	5,108	2,542	712	1,830	3,278
13	6,955	1,947	5,008	1,716	480	1,236	3,772
14	6,802	1,905	4,897	805	225	580	4,317
15	6,632	1,857	4,775	42	12	30	4,745
16	6,444	1,804	4,640				4,640
17	6,236	1,746	4,490				4,490
18	6,007	1,682	4,325				4,325
19	5,754	1,611	4,143				4,143
20	5,475	1,533	3,942				3,942
21	5,166	1,446	3,720				3,720
22	4,824	1,351	3,473				3,473
23	4,447	1,245	3,202				3,202
24	4,031	1,129	2,902				2,902
25	3,571	1,000	2,571				2,571
26	3,063	858	2,205				2,205
27	2,501	700	1,801				1,801
28	1,881	527	1,354				1,354
29	1,195	335	860				860
30	438	123	315				315
Total	$172,734	$48,366	$124,368	$69,671	$19,509	$50,162	$74,206

Remaining Balances

Year	30 Years	15 Years	$100 Per Month	$200 Per Month	$1,000 Per Year	$2,000 Per Year
1	$ 8,424.72	$ 10,316.28	$ 9,624.72	$ 10,824.72	$ 9,424.72	$ 10,424.72
2	8,424.72	10,316.28	9,624.72	10,824.72	9,424.72	10,424.72
3	8,424.72	10,316.28	9,624.72	10,824.72	9,424.72	10,424.72
4	8,424.72	10,316.28	9,624.72	10,824.72	9,424.72	10,424.72
5	8,424.72	10,316.28	9,624.72	10,824.72	9,424.72	10,424.72
6	8,424.72	10,316.28	9,624.72	10,824.72	9,424.72	10,424.72
7	8,424.72	10,316.28	9,624.72	10,824.72	9,424.72	10,424.72
8	8,424.72	10,316.28	9,624.72	10,824.72	9,424.72	10,424.72
9	8,424.72	10,316.28	9,624.72	10,824.72	9,424.72	10,424.72
10	8,424.72	10,316.28	9,624.72	10,824.72	9,424.72	10,424.72
11	8,424.72	10,316.28	9,624.72	10,824.72	9,424.72	10,424.72
12	8,424.72	10,316.28	9,624.72	10,824.72	9,424.72	10,424.72
13	8,424.72	10,316.28	9,624.72	10,824.72	9,424.72	10,424.72
14	8,424.72	10,316.28	9,624.72	5,306.00	9,424.72	10,424.72
15	8,424.72	10,316.06	9,624.72		9,424.72	3,724.97
16	8,424.72		9,624.72		9,424.72	
17	8,424.72		9,624.72		9,424.72	
18	8,424.72		8,316.55		9,424.72	
19	8,424.72				6,593.00	
20	8,424.72					
21	8,424.72					
22	8,424.72					
23	8,424.72					
24	8,424.72					
25	8,424.72					
26	8,424.72					
27	8,424.72					
28	8,424.72					
29	8,424.72					
30	8,424.78					
Total	$252,734.66	$154,743.98	$171,936.79	$146,027.36	$176,237.96	$149,671.05
Principal	80,000.00	80,000.00	80,000.00	80,000.00	80,000.00	80,000.00
Interest	$172,734.66	$ 74,743.98	$ 91,936.79	$ 66,027.36	$ 96,237.96	$ 69,671.05

Remaining Balances (Continued)

Year	30 Years	15 Years	$100 Per Month	$200 Per Month	$1,000 Per Year	$2,000 Per Year
1	99.4%	97.0%	97.9%	96.3%	98.1%	96.7%
2	98.8	93.6	95.5	92.2	95.9	93.1
3	98.2	89.9	92.9	87.7	93.6	89.0
4	97.4	85.8	90.1	82.7	91.0	84.6
5	96.6	81.3	86.9	77.2	88.1	79.7
6	95.7	76.3	83.4	71.1	85.0	74.3
7	94.6	70.8	79.5	64.4	81.5	68.3
8	93.5	64.7	75.3	57.0	77.6	61.7
9	92.3	58.0	70.5	48.8	73.3	54.4
10	90.9	50.6	65.3	39.7	68.6	46.3
11	89.4	42.4	59.6	29.7	63.4	37.4
12	87.8	33.3	53.2	18.7	57.6	27.5
13	85.9	23.3	46.2	6.4	51.3	16.6
14	83.9	12.2	38.4	0	44.3	4.6
15	81.7	0	29.9		36.5	0
16	79.2		20.4		27.9	
17	76.5		9.9		18.4	
18	73.4		0		8.0	
19	70.1				0	
20	66.4					
21	62.3					
22	57.8					
23	52.9					
24	47.4					
25	41.3					
26	34.6					
27	27.2					
28	19.0					
29	10.0					
30	0					

GRADUATING PAYMENT PLANS

This second main section compares mortgage acceleration plans that involve annual increases in payments. Each example is based on an $80,000 loan at 10 percent interest. The plans presented include

1. *Full Amortization, 30 Years.* This summary shows the cost of paying a loan without any form of acceleration.

2. *Increase Payments by $25 Each Year.* Under this plan, the required monthly payment is increased at the beginning of each year by $25 per month. As each new year begins, an additional $25 is added to the total payment, and the increases are continued each year.

3. *Increase Payments by $50 Each Year.* This idea is similar to the preceding plan, except that each year's payments are increased by $50 at the beginning of each year. However, no increase occurs during the first year. And from the fifth year forward, payments are leveled out at $902.06 per month.

4. *Double Each Month's Principal.* Under this plan, the total payment grows each month. Beginning with the minimum required payment with 30-year amortization, the monthly interest is calculated and deducted from that total. The remaining principal is then doubled. For example, in the first month, $702.06 is the required payment. Interest on $80,000 is $666.67. The balance, $35.39, would be assigned to principal under a fully amortized schedule. However, that amount is doubled to $70.78, and the total payment increases to $737.15.

1. Full Amortization, 30 Years

Year	Total Payments	Paid to Interest	Paid to Principal	Balance
				$80,000.00
1	$ 8,424.72	$ 7,979.97	$ 444.75	79,555.25
2	8,424.72	7,933.40	491.32	79,063.93
3	8,424.72	7,881.98	542.74	78,521.19
4	8,424.72	7,825.12	599.60	77,921.59
5	8,424.72	7,762.36	662.36	77,259.23
6	8,424.72	7,692.98	731.74	76,527.49
7	8,424.72	7,616.35	808.37	75,719.12
8	8,424.72	7,531.69	893.03	74,826.09
9	8,424.72	7,438.20	986.52	73,839.57
10	8,424.72	7,334.91	1,089.81	72,749.76
11	8,424.72	7,220.79	1,203.93	71,545.83
12	8,424.72	7,094.72	1,330.00	70,215.83
13	8,424.72	6,955.46	1,469.26	68,746.57
14	8,424.72	6,801.60	1,623.12	67,123.45
15	8,424.72	6,631.64	1,793.08	65,330.37
16	8,424.72	6,443.88	1,980.84	63,349.53
17	8,424.72	6,236.45	2,188.27	61,161.26
18	8,424.72	6,007.33	2,417.39	58,743.87
19	8,424.72	5,754.18	2,670.54	56,073.33
20	8,424.72	5,474.54	2,950.18	53,123.15
21	8,424.72	5,165.61	3,259.11	49,864.04
22	8,424.72	4,824.36	3,600.36	46,263.68
23	8,424.72	4,447.34	3,977.38	42,286.30
24	8,424.72	4,030.85	4,393.87	37,892.43
25	8,424.72	3,570.77	4,853.95	33,038.48
26	8,424.72	3,062.50	5,362.22	27,676.26
27	8,424.72	2,501.02	5,923.70	21,752.56
28	8,424.72	1,880.70	6,544.02	15,208.54
29	8,424.72	1,195.48	7,229.24	7,979.30
30	8,417.78	438.48	7,979.30	0
Total	$252,734.66	$172,734.66	$80,000.00	

2. Increase Payments by $25 Each Year

Year	Total Payments	Paid to Interest	Paid to Principal	Balance
				$80,000.00
1	$ 8,724.72	$ 7,965.83	$ 758.89	79,241.11
2	9,024.72	7,872.26	1,152.46	78,088.65
3	9,324.72	7,737.42	1,587.30	76,501.35
4	9,624.72	7,557.07	2,067.65	74,433.70
5	9,924.72	7,326.43	2,598.29	71,835.41
6	10,224.72	7,040.21	3,184.51	68,650.90
7	10,524.72	6,692.61	3,832.11	64,818.79
8	10,824.72	6,277.18	4,547.54	62,271.25
9	11,124.72	5,786.86	5,337.86	54,933.39
10	11,424.72	5,213.80	6,210.92	48,722.47
11	11,724.72	4,549.30	7,175.42	41,547.05
12	12,024.72	3,783.80	8,240.92	33,306.13
13	12,324.72	2,906.73	9,417.99	23,888.14
14	12,624.72	1,906.22	10,718.50	13,169.64
15	12,924.72	769.90	12,154.82	1,014.82
16	1,099.39	84.57	1,014.82	0
Total	$163,470.19	$83,470.19	$80,000.00	

3. Increase Payments by $50 Each Year

Year	Total Payments	Paid to Interest	Paid to Principal	Balance
				$80,000.00
1	$ 8,424.72	$ 7,979.97	$ 444.75	79,555.25
2	9,024.72	7,905.12	1,119.60	78,435.65
3	9,624.72	7,759.61	1,865.11	76,570.54
4	10,224.72	7,536.03	2,688.69	73,881.85
5	10,824.72	7,226.21	3,598.51	70,283.34
6	10,824.72	6,849.41	3,975.31	66,308.03
7	10,824.72	6,433.14	4,391.58	61,916.45
8	10,824.72	5,973.29	4,851.43	57,065.02
9	10,824.72	5,465.28	5,359.44	51,705.58
10	10,824.72	4,904.07	5,920.65	45,784.93

3. Increase Payments by $50 Each Year (Continued)

Year	Total Payments	Paid to Interest	Paid to Principal	Balance
11	10,824.72	4,284.11	6,540.61	39,244.32
12	10,824.72	3,599.20	7,225.52	32,018.80
13	10,824.72	2,842.61	7,982.11	24,036.69
14	10,824.72	2,006.78	8,817.94	15,218.75
15	10,824.72	1,083.41	9,741.31	5,477.44
16	5,644.99	167.55	5,477.44	0
Total	$162,015.79	$82,015.79	$80,000.00	

4. Double Each Month's Principal

Year	Total Payments	Paid to Interest	Paid to Principal	Balance
				$80,000.00
1	$ 8,890.59	$ 7,958.85	$ 931.74	79,068.26
2	8,992.84	7,856.60	1,136.24	77,932.02
3	9,117.47	7,731.97	1,385.50	76,546.52
4	9,269.44	7,580.00	1,689.44	74,857.08
5	9,454.77	7,394.67	2,060.10	72,796.98
6	9,680.77	7,168.67	2,512.10	70,284.88
7	9,956.32	6,893.12	3,063.20	67,221.68
8	10,292.34	6,557.10	3,735.24	63,486.44
9	10,702.08	6,147.36	4,554.72	58,931.72
10	11,201.72	5,647.72	5,554.00	53,377.72
11	11,810.96	5,038.48	6,772.48	46,605.24
12	12,553.87	4,295.57	8,258.30	38,346.94
13	13,459.78	3,389.66	10,070.12	28,276.82
14	14,564.41	2,285.03	12,279.38	15,997.44
15	15,911.41	938.03	14,973.38	1,024.06
16	1,032.59	8.53	1,024.06	0
Total	$166,891.36	$86,891.36	$80,000.00	

After-Tax Interest Cost

The three schedules that follow (pp. 215–217) compare plans for graduating payments on an after-tax basis. The assumption is made that the effective tax rate in each case will be 28 percent.

These schedules show how each plan of acceleration decreases the cost of buying your home, after the benefit of deducting mortgage interest has been calculated.

Cash Payments

The schedule on page 218 summarizes the total of cash payments that will be made under various repayment plans. This comparison will assist you in evaluating both the annual cost of a mortgage and the total interest savings.

After-Tax Interest Cost: Increase Payments by $25 Each Year

	Full Amortization			With Acceleration			
Year	Interest	Tax Savings	After-Tax Cost	Interest	Tax Savings	After-Tax Cost	Net Saved
1	$ 7,980	$ 2,234	$ 5,746	$ 7,966	$ 2,230	$ 5,736	$ 10
2	7,933	2,221	5,712	7,872	2,204	5,668	44
3	7,882	2,207	5,675	7,737	2,166	5,571	104
4	7,825	2,191	5,634	7,557	2,116	5,441	193
5	7,762	2,173	5,589	7,326	2,051	5,275	314
6	7,693	2,154	5,539	7,040	1,971	5,069	470
7	7,616	2,132	5,484	6,692	1,874	4,818	666
8	7,532	2,109	5,423	6,277	1,758	4,519	904
9	7,438	2,083	5,355	5,787	1,620	4,167	1,188
10	7,335	2,054	5,281	5,214	1,460	3,754	1,527
11	7,221	2,022	5,199	4,549	1,274	3,275	1,924
12	7,095	1,987	5,108	3,784	1,060	2,724	2,384
13	6,955	1,947	5,008	2,907	814	2,093	2,915
14	6,802	1,905	4,897	1,906	534	1,372	3,525
15	6,632	1,857	4,775	770	216	554	4,221
16	6,444	1,804	4,640	85	24	61	4,579
17	6,236	1,746	4,490				4,490
18	6,007	1,682	4,325				4,325
19	5,754	1,611	4,143				4,143
20	5,475	1,533	3,942				3,942
21	5,166	1,446	3,720				3,720
22	4,824	1,351	3,473				3,473
23	4,447	1,245	3,202				3,202
24	4,031	1,129	2,902				2,902
25	3,571	1,000	2,571				2,571
26	3,063	858	2,205				2,205
27	2,501	700	1,801				1,801
28	1,881	527	1,354				1,354
29	1,195	335	860				860
30	438	123	315				315
Total	$172,734	$48,366	$124,368	$83,469	$23,372	$60,097	$64,271

After-Tax Interest Cost: Increase Payments by $50 Each Year

	Full Amortization			With Acceleration			
Year	Interest	Tax Savings	After-Tax Cost	Interest	Tax Savings	After-Tax Cost	Net Saved
1	$ 7,980	$ 2,234	$ 5,746	$ 7,980	$ 2,234	$ 5,746	$ 0
2	7,933	2,221	5,712	7,905	2,213	5,692	20
3	7,882	2,207	5,675	7,760	2,173	5,587	88
4	7,825	2,191	5,634	7,536	2,110	5,426	208
5	7,762	2,173	5,589	7,226	2,023	5,203	386
6	7,693	2,154	5,539	6,849	1,918	4,931	608
7	7,616	2,132	5,484	6,433	1,801	4,632	852
8	7,532	2,109	5,423	5,973	1,672	4,301	1,122
9	7,438	2,083	5,355	5,465	1,530	3,935	1,420
10	7,335	2,054	5,281	4,904	1,373	3,531	1,750
11	7,221	2,022	5,199	4,284	1,200	3,084	2,115
12	7,095	1,987	5,108	3,599	1,008	2,591	2,517
13	6,955	1,947	5,008	2,843	796	2,047	2,961
14	6,802	1,905	4,897	2,007	562	1,445	3,452
15	6,632	1,857	4,775	1,083	303	780	3,995
16	6,444	1,804	4,640	168	47	121	4,519
17	6,236	1,746	4,490				4,490
18	6,007	1,682	4,325				4,325
19	5,754	1,611	4,143				4,143
20	5,475	1,533	3,942				3,942
21	5,166	1,446	3,720				3,720
22	4,824	1,351	3,473				3,473
23	4,447	1,245	3,202				3,202
24	4,031	1,129	2,902				2,902
25	3,571	1,000	2,571				2,571
26	3,063	858	2,205				2,205
27	2,501	700	1,801				1,801
28	1,881	527	1,354				1,354
29	1,195	335	860				860
30	438	123	315				315
Total	$172,734	$48,366	$124,368	$82,015	$22,963	$59,052	$65,316

After-Tax Interest Cost: Double Each Month's Principal

Year	Full Amortization			With Acceleration			
	Interest	Tax Savings	After-Tax Cost	Interest	Tax Savings	After-Tax Cost	Net Saved
1	$ 7,980	$ 2,234	$ 5,746	$ 7,959	$ 2,229	$ 5,730	$ 16
2	7,933	2,221	5,712	7,857	2,200	5,657	55
3	7,882	2,207	5,675	7,732	2,165	5,567	108
4	7,825	2,191	5,634	7,580	2,122	5,458	176
5	7,762	2,173	5,589	7,395	2,071	5,324	265
6	7,693	2,154	5,539	7,169	2,007	5,162	377
7	7,616	2,132	5,484	6,893	1,930	4,963	521
8	7,532	2,109	5,423	6,557	1,836	4,721	702
9	7,438	2,083	5,355	6,147	1,721	4,426	929
10	7,335	2,054	5,281	5,648	1,581	4,067	1,214
11	7,221	2,022	5,199	5,038	1,411	3,627	1,572
12	7,095	1,987	5,108	4,296	1,203	3,093	2,015
13	6,955	1,947	5,008	3,390	949	2,441	2,567
14	6,802	1,905	4,897	2,285	640	1,645	3,252
15	6,632	1,857	4,775	938	263	675	4,100
16	6,444	1,804	4,640	9	3	6	4,634
17	6,236	1,746	4,490				4,490
18	6,007	1,682	4,325				4,325
19	5,754	1,611	4,143				4,143
20	5,475	1,533	3,942				3,942
21	5,166	1,446	3,720				3,720
22	4,824	1,351	3,473				3,473
23	4,447	1,245	3,202				3,202
24	4,031	1,129	2,902				2,902
25	3,571	1,000	2,571				2,571
26	3,063	858	2,205				2,205
27	2,501	700	1,801				1,801
28	1,881	527	1,354				1,354
29	1,195	335	860				860
30	438	123	315				315
Total	$172,734	$48,366	$124,368	$86,893	$24,331	$62,562	$61,806

Cash Payments

Year	30 Years	$25 Per Year	$50 Per Year	Double Principal
1	$ 8,424.72	$ 8,724.72	$ 8,424.72	$ 8,890.59
2	8,424.72	9,024.72	9,024.72	8,992.84
3	8,424.72	9,324.72	9,624.72	9,117.47
4	8,424.72	9,624.72	10,224.72	9,269.44
5	8,424.72	9,924.72	10,824.72	9,454.77
6	8,424.72	10,224.72	10,824.72	9,680.77
7	8,424.72	10,524.72	10,824.72	9,956.32
8	8,424.72	10,824.72	10,824.72	10,292.34
9	8,424.72	11,124.72	10,824.72	10,702.08
10	8,424.72	11,424.72	10,824.72	11,201.72
11	8,424.72	11,724.72	10,824.72	11,810.96
12	8,424.72	12,024.72	10,824.72	12,553.87
13	8,424.72	12,324.72	10,824.72	13,459.78
14	8,424.72	12,624.72	10,824.72	14,564.41
15	8,424.72	12,924.72	10,824.72	15,911,41
16	8,424.72	1,099.39	5,644.99	1,032.59
17	8,424.72			
18	8,424.72			
19	8,424.72			
20	8,424.72			
21	8,424.72			
22	8,424.72			
23	8,424.72			
24	8,424.72			
25	8,424.72			
26	8,424.72			
27	8,424.72			
28	8,424.72			
29	8,424.72			
30	8,417.78			
Total	$252,734.66	$163,470.19	$162,015.79	$166,891.36
Principal	80,000.00	80,000.00	80,000.00	80,000.00
Interest	$172,734.66	$ 83,470.19	$ 82,015.79	$ 86,891.36

Remaining Balances

The next schedule summarizes the remaining balances outstanding on loans under the different graduating repayment plans.

Remaining balance is the percentage of the original loan that remains due at the end of each year. This schedule will help you compare the rate of acceleration of the different plans.

Remaining Balances

Year	30 Years	$25 Per Year	$50 Per Year	Double Principal
1	99.4%	99.1%	99.4%	98.8%
2	98.4	97.6	98.0	97.4
3	98.2	95.6	95.7	95.7
4	97.4	93.0	92.4	93.6
5	96.6	89.8	87.9	91.0
6	95.7	85.8	82.9	87.9
7	94.6	81.0	77.4	84.0
8	93.5	75.3	71.3	79.4
9	92.3	68.7	64.6	73.7
10	90.9	60.9	57.2	66.7
11	89.4	51.9	49.1	58.3
12	87.8	41.6	40.0	47.9
13	85.9	29.9	30.0	35.3
14	83.9	16.5	19.0	20.0
15	81.7	1.3	6.8	1.3
16	79.2	0	0	0
17	76.5			
18	73.4			
19	70.1			
20	66.4			
21	62.3			
22	57.8			
23	52.9			
24	47.4			
25	41.3			
26	34.6			
27	27.2			
28	19.0			
29	10.0			
30	0			

VARIABLE LOAN PLANS

This third main section of the appendix compares mortgage acceleration strategies that can be used when the loan contains a variable interest rate. To make the comparison valid, the following assumptions have been made:

1. The loan is for $80,000 and contains a provision for 30-year amortization.

2. The initial interest rate is 8 percent, and the lender will increase that rate by 1 percent per year, to the maximum of 13 percent.

With the latter assumption in mind, the interest rate as calculated for the first six years under each plan will increase on the following schedule:

Year	Rate
1	8%
2	9
3	10
4	11
5	12
6–on	13

The following plans are presented:

1. *Full Amortization.* The amount of each month's payment is calculated based on a 30-year amortization rate. Because a portion of the principal will have been paid at the time a new rate takes effect, the repayment schedule will be completed in the 28th year.

Depending on the practice of a lender, the new monthly payment may be calculated in this way or based on the amount necessary to amortize the current balance over the remainder of the 30-year period.

2. *15-Year Amortization.* Payments are increased at each rate of interest to amortize the loan over a 15-year term.

3. *Pay $885 Per Month.* This form of acceleration calls for paying the maximum rate the lender could charge, at the highest rate of interest possible under terms of the loan. Because that maximum rate will not be reached for several years, this plan has the effect of prepaying a substantial portion of the principal during the early years.

4. *Principal Offset Plan.* Under this arrangement, the monthly payment reflects the amount that would be due if the rate were 1 percent higher. This plan assumes that the lender is allowed by contract to raise the rate by 1 percent per year. When the effective rate is 8 percent, payment is made at the level required for 9 percent; when the lender raises the rate to 9 percent, the payment is accelerated to the level required at 10 percent. This procedure continues until the effective rate is 13 percent. At that point, payments are frozen at $936.31, which is $11.59 per month lower than the rate that would be charged at 14 percent.

1. Full Amortization

Year	Total Payments	Paid to Interest	Paid to Principal	Balance
				$80,000.00
1	$ 7,044.24	$ 6,375.84	$ 668.40	$79,331.60
2	7,724.40	7,115.11	609.29	78,722.31
3	8,424.72	7,846.22	578.50	78,143.81
4	9,142.32	8,567.41	574.91	77,568.90
5	9,874.80	9,276.05	598.75	76,970.15
6	10,619.52	9,968.21	651.31	76,318.84
7	10,619.52	9,878.33	741.19	75,577.65
8	10,619.52	9,776.02	843.50	74,734.15
9	10,619.52	9,659.58	959.94	73,774.21
10	10,619.52	9,527.05	1,092.47	72,681.74
11	10,619.52	9,376.28	1,243.24	71,438.50
12	10,619.52	9,204.67	1,414.85	70,023.65
13	10,619.52	9,009.37	1,610.15	68,413.50
14	10,619.52	8,787.12	1,832.40	66,581.10
15	10,619.52	8,534.20	2,085.32	64,495.78
16	10,619.52	8,246.36	2,373.16	62,122.62
17	10,619.52	7,918.78	2,700.74	59,421.88
18	10,619.52	7,545.97	2,073.55	56,348.33
19	10,619.52	7,121.74	3,497.78	52,850.55
20	10,619.52	6,638.90	3,980.62	48,869.93
21	10,619.52	6,089.46	4,530.06	44,339.87
22	10,619.52	5,464.19	5,155.33	39,184.54
23	10,619.52	4,752.59	5,866.93	33,317.61
24	10,619.52	3,942.74	6,676.78	26,640.83
25	10,619.52	3,021.14	7,598.38	19,042.45
26	10,619.52	1,972.31	8,647.21	10,395.24
27	10,619.52	778.72	9,840.80	554.44
28	560.45	6.01	554.44	0
Total	$276,400.37	$196,400.37	$80,000.00	

2. 15-Year Amortization

Year	Total Payments	Paid to Interest	Paid to Principal	Balance
				$80,000.00
1	$ 9,174.36	$ 6,295.67	$ 2,878.69	77,121.31
2	9,737.04	6,822.65	2,914.39	74,206.92
3	10,316.28	7,284.23	3,032.05	71,174.87
4	10,911.36	7,669.02	3,242.34	67,932.53
5	11,521.68	7,960.26	3,561.42	64,371.11
6	12,146.40	8,134.80	4,011.60	60,359.51
7	12,146.40	7,581.05	4,565.35	55,794.16
8	12,146.40	6,950.91	5,195.49	50,598.67
9	12,146.40	6,233.77	5,912.63	44,686.04
10	12,146.40	5,417.63	6,728.77	37,957.27
11	12,146.40	4,488.83	7,657.57	30,299.70
12	12,146.40	3,431.84	8,714.56	21,585.14
13	12,146.40	2,228.95	9,917.45	11,667.69
14	12,146.40	860.01	11,286.39	381.30
15	385.43	4.13	381.30	0
Total	$161,363.75	$81,363.75	$80,000.00	

3. Pay $885 per Month

Year	Total Payments	Paid to Interest	Paid to Principal	Balance
				$80,000.00
1	$ 10,620.00	$ 6,241.76	$ 4,378.24	75,621.76
2	10,620.00	6,644.62	3,975.38	71,646.38
3	10,620.00	7,001.76	3,618.24	68,028.14
4	10,620.00	7,320.02	3,299.98	64,728.16
5	10,620.00	7,605.14	3,014.86	61,713.30
6	10,620.00	7,862.27	2,757.73	58,955.57
7	10,620.00	7,481.60	3,138.40	55,817.17
8	10,620.00	7,048.40	3,571.60	52,245.57
9	10,620.00	6,555.39	4,064.61	48,180.96
10	10,620.00	5,994.35	4,625.65	43,555.31

3. Pay $885 per Month (Continued)

Year	Total Payments	Paid to Interest	Paid to Principal	Balance
11	10,620.00	5,355.87	5,264.13	38,291.18
12	10,620.00	4,629.24	5,990.76	32,300.42
13	10,620.00	3,802.30	6,817.70	25,482.72
14	10,620.00	2,861.25	7,758.75	17,723.97
15	10,620.00	1,790.29	8,829.71	8,894.26
16	9,468.63	574.37	8,894.26	0
Total	$168,768.63	$88,768.63	$80,000.00	

4. Principal Offset Plan

Year	Total Payments	Paid to Interest	Paid to Principal	Balance
				$80,000.00
1	$ 7,724.40	$ 6,350.34	$ 1,374.06	78,625.94
2	8,424.72	7,019.30	1,405.42	77,220.52
3	9,142.32	7,655.11	1,487.21	75,733.31
4	9,874.80	8,250.39	1,624.41	74,108.90
5	10,619.52	8,794.89	1,824.63	72,284.27
6	11,235.72	9,283.37	1,952.35	70,331.92
7	11,235.72	9,013.86	2,221.86	68,110.06
8	11,235.72	8,707.17	2,528.55	65,581.51
9	11,235.72	8,358.15	2,877.57	62,703.94
10	11,235.72	7,960.94	3,274.78	59,429.16
11	11,235.72	7,508.92	3,726.80	55,702.36
12	11,235.72	6,995.51	4,241.21	51,461.15
13	11,235.72	6,409.08	4,826.64	46,634.51
14	11,235.72	5,742.84	5,492.88	41,141.63
15	11,235.72	4,984.63	6,251.09	34,890.54
16	11,235.72	4,121.79	7,113.93	27,776.61
17	11,235.72	3,139.83	8,095.89	19,680.72
18	11,235.72	2,022.34	9,213.38	10,467.34
19	11,217.94	750.60	10,467.34	0
Total	$203,068.06	$123,068.06	$80,000.00	

After-Tax Interest Cost

The next series of schedules (pp. 226–228) shows how each acceleration plan compares with full amortization. This summary assumes

A variable rate applies, ranging from 8 to 13 percent with a 1 percent increase each year
An effective federal tax rate of 28 percent

Each schedule reports the total interest cost by year, followed by the tax savings and the net after-tax interest cost. The last column shows the amount saved each year with the acceleration plan.

Cash Payments

The schedule on page 229 shows the level of total payments made each year and for each of the variable-rate plans.

Increases occur due to increased interest rates until the maximum contracted rate is reached. In all cases, the beginning rate is 8 percent; that rate is raised by 1 percent per year, and it is frozen when the assumed maximum rate of 13 percent has been reached.

After-Tax Interest Cost: 15-Year Amortization

	Full Amortization			With Acceleration			
Year	Interest	Tax Savings	After-Tax Cost	Interest	Tax Savings	After-Tax Cost	Net Saved
1	$ 6,376	$ 1,785	$ 4,591	$ 6,296	$ 1,763	$ 4,533	$ 58
2	7,115	1,992	5,123	6,823	1,910	4,913	210
3	7,846	2,197	5,649	7,284	2,040	5,244	405
4	8,567	2,399	6,168	7,669	2,147	5,522	646
5	9,276	2,597	6,679	7,960	2,229	5,731	948
6	9,968	2,791	7,177	8,135	2,278	5,857	1,320
7	9,878	2,766	7,112	7,581	2,123	5,458	1,654
8	9,776	2,737	7,039	6,951	1,946	5,005	2,034
9	9,660	2,705	6,955	6,234	1,746	4,488	2,467
10	9,527	2,668	6,859	5,418	1,517	3,901	2,958
11	9,376	2,625	6,751	4,489	1,257	3,232	3,519
12	9,205	2,577	6,628	3,432	961	2,471	4,157
13	9,009	2,523	6,486	2,229	624	1,605	4,881
14	8,787	2,460	6,327	860	241	619	5,708
15	8,534	2,390	6,144	4	1	3	6,141
16	8,246	2,309	5,937				5,937
17	7,919	2,217	5,702				5,702
18	7,546	2,113	5,433				5,433
19	7,122	1,994	5,128				5,128
20	6,639	1,859	4,780				4,780
21	6,089	1,705	4,384				4,384
22	5,464	1,530	3,934				3,934
23	4,753	1,331	3,422				3,422
24	3,943	1,104	2,839				2,839
25	3,021	846	2,175				2,175
26	1,972	552	1,420				1,420
27	779	218	561				561
28	6	2	4				4
Total	$196,399	$54,992	$141,407	$81,365	$22,783	$58,582	$82,825

After-Tax Interest Cost: Pay $885 Per Month

	Full Amortization			With Acceleration			
Year	Interest	Tax Savings	After-Tax Cost	Interest	Tax Savings	After-Tax Cost	Net Saved
1	$ 6,376	$ 1,785	$ 4,591	$ 6,242	$ 1,748	$ 4,494	$ 97
2	7,115	1,992	5,123	6,645	1,861	4,784	339
3	7,846	2,197	5,649	7,002	1,961	5,041	608
4	8,567	2,399	6,168	7,320	2,050	5,270	898
5	9,276	2,597	6,679	7,605	2,129	5,476	1,203
6	9,968	2,791	7,177	7,862	2,201	5,661	1,516
7	9,878	2,766	7,112	7,482	2,095	5,387	1,725
8	9,776	2,737	7,039	7,048	1,973	5,075	1,964
9	9,660	2,705	6,955	6,555	1,835	4,720	2,235
10	9,527	2,668	6,859	5,994	1,678	4,316	2,543
11	9,376	2,625	6,751	5,356	1,500	3,856	2,895
12	9,205	2,577	6,628	4,629	1,296	3,333	3,295
13	9,009	2,523	6,486	3,802	1,065	2,737	3,749
14	8,787	2,460	6,327	2,861	801	2,060	4,267
15	8,534	2,390	6,144	1,790	501	1,289	4,855
16	8,246	2,309	5,937	574	161	413	5,524
17	7,919	2,217	5,702				5,702
18	7,546	2,113	5,433				5,433
19	7,122	1,994	5,128				5,128
20	6,639	1,859	4,780				4,780
21	6,089	1,705	4,384				4,384
22	5,464	1,530	3,934				3,934
23	4,753	1,331	3,422				3,422
24	3,943	1,104	2,839				2,839
25	3,021	846	2,175				2,175
26	1,972	552	1,420				1,420
27	779	218	561				561
28	6	2	4				4
Total	$196,399	$54,992	$141,407	$88,767	$24,855	$63,912	$77,495

After-Tax Interest Cost: Principal Offset Plan

	Full Amortization			With Acceleration			
Year	Interest	Tax Savings	After-Tax Cost	Interest	Tax Savings	After-Tax Cost	Net Saved
1	$ 6,376	$ 1,785	$ 4,591	$ 6,350	$ 1,778	$ 4,572	$ 19
2	7,115	1,992	5,123	7,019	1,965	5,054	69
3	7,846	2,197	5,649	7,655	2,143	5,512	137
4	8,567	2,399	6,168	8,250	2,310	5,940	228
5	9,276	2,597	6,679	8,795	2,463	6,332	347
6	9,968	2,791	7,177	9,283	2,599	6,684	493
7	9,878	2,766	7,112	9,014	2,524	6,490	622
8	9,776	2,737	7,039	8,707	2,438	6,269	770
9	9,660	2,705	6,955	8,358	2,340	6,018	937
10	9,527	2,668	6,859	7,961	2,229	5,732	1,127
11	9,376	2,625	6,751	7,509	2,103	5,406	1,345
12	9,205	2,577	6,628	6,995	1,959	5,036	1,592
13	9,009	2,523	6,486	6,409	1,795	4,614	1,872
14	8,787	2,460	6,327	5,743	1,608	4,135	2,192
15	8,534	2,390	6,144	4,985	1,396	3,589	2,555
16	8,246	2,309	5,937	4,122	1,154	2,968	2,969
17	7,919	2,217	5,702	3,140	879	2,261	3,441
18	7,546	2,113	5,433	2,022	566	1,456	3,977
19	7,122	1,994	5,128	751	210	541	4,587
20	6,639	1,859	4,780				4,780
21	6,089	1,705	4,384				4,384
22	5,464	1,530	3,934				3,934
23	4,753	1,331	3,422				3,422
24	3,943	1,104	2,839				2,839
25	3,021	846	2,175				2,175
26	1,972	552	1,420				1,420
27	779	218	561				561
28	6	2	4				4
Total	$196,399	$54,992	$141,407	$123,068	$34,459	$88,609	$52,798

Cash Payments

Year	30 Years	15 Years	$885 Per Month	Principal Offset
1	$ 7,044.24	$ 9,174.36	$ 10,620.00	$ 7,724.40
2	7,724.40	9,737.04	10,620.00	8,424.72
3	8,424.72	10,316.28	10,620.00	9,142.32
4	9,142.32	10,911.36	10,620.00	9,874.80
5	9,874.80	11,521.68	10,620.00	10,619.52
6	10,619.52	12,146.40	10,620.00	11,235.72
7	10,619.52	12,146.40	10,620.00	11,235.72
8	10,619.52	12,146.40	10,620.00	11,235.72
9	10,619.52	12,146.40	10,620.00	11,235.72
10	10,619.52	12,146.40	10,620.00	11,235.72
11	10,619.52	12,146.40	10,620.00	11,235.72
12	10,619.52	12,146.40	10,620.00	11,235.72
13	10,619.52	12,146.40	10,620.00	11,235.72
14	10,619.52	12,146.40	10,620.00	11,235.72
15	10,619.52	385.43	10,620.00	11,235.72
16	10,619.52		9,468.63	11,235.72
17	10,619.52			11,235.72
18	10,619.52			11,235.72
19	10,619.52			11,217.94
20	10,619.52			
21	10,619.52			
22	10,619.52			
23	10,619.52			
24	10,619.52			
25	10,619.52			
26	10,619.52			
27	10,619.52			
28	560.45			
Total	$276,400.37	$161,363.75	$168,768.63	$203,068.06
Principal	80,000.00	80,000.00	80,000.00	80,000.00
Interest	$196,400.37	$ 81,363.75	$ 88,768.63	$123,068.06

Remaining Balances

The next summary table shows the percentage of the loan that remains due at the end of each year. Even with some forms of acceleration, the rate declines slowly during the early years, because of the offsetting increases in the effective interest rate under the variable-rate contract.

This schedule enables you to compare total costs and the rate of amortization under each of the variable-rate plans.

Remaining Balances

Year	30 Years	15 Years	$885 Per Month	Principal Offset
1	99.2%	96.4%	94.5%	98.3%
2	98.4	92.8	89.6	96.5
3	97.7	89.0	85.0	94.7
4	97.0	84.9	80.9	92.6
5	96.2	80.5	77.1	90.4
6	95.4	75.4	73.7	87.9
7	94.5	69.7	69.8	85.1
8	93.4	63.2	65.3	82.0
9	92.2	55.9	60.2	78.4
10	90.8	47.4	54.4	74.3
11	89.3	37.9	47.9	69.6
12	87.5	27.0	40.4	64.3
13	85.5	14.6	31.9	58.3
14	83.2	0.5	22.2	51.4
15	80.6	0	11.1	43.6
16	77.7		0	34.7
17	74.3			24.6
18	70.4			13.1
19	66.1			0
20	61.1			
21	55.4			
22	49.0			
23	41.6			
24	33.3			
25	23.8			
26	13.0			
27	7.7			
28	0			

GLOSSARY

addition (1) An improvement made to a residence or other property to increase living space, remodel an existing room, or add other permanent features. (2) An extra amount added to monthly payments to increase principal and reduce overall interest expense.

adjustable-rate mortgage A mortgage in which an initial lower-than-market rate is increased periodically. Limitations on the amount of increase are applied both to the annual increase and the maximum that can be charged during the term of the loan.

adjusted basis The cost of property, plus closing costs and improvements, and minus any claimed depreciation for rental or home office use.

adjusted sales price The agreed-upon sales price of property, minus commissions and closing costs paid, and minus any qualified fixing-up expenses paid in anticipation of the sale.

after-tax profit The gain realized after allowing for tax benefits or deductions. For example, an acceleration plan reduces interest over the period of a loan. However, that gain is reduced when the benefits of itemized deductions are calculated.

amortization The process of repaying a loan. Under most mortgage contracts, a recurring monthly payment is made, with a portion assigned to interest (computed on the basis of the loan's balance) and the remainder assigned to principal.

amortization table A table that shows the amount of monthly payment required to repay a loan, given a specific rate of interest, a loan amount, and the number of years in the term. An amortization table may report information in one of two ways. An *amount* table shows the actual monthly payment at various loan levels. A *factor* table reports the amount per $1 that must be paid for a number of years.

annual compounding A method of compounding interest only once per year. Compounding will occur at the stated rate of interest. For example, a $2,000 loan subject to 10 percent interest, compounded annually, will include first-year interest of $200. In the second year, interest is computed on the new balance of $2,200. Interest (assuming no repayments have been made) is $220.

balloon mortgage Also called a rollover mortgage or renegotiable rate mortgage; a form of loan in which periodic payments are made for interest only or for interest and minimum principal payments. At the end of a stated term, the entire loan balance becomes due.

buy-down mortgage A mortgage in which the borrower buys a home from a developer and is allowed to pay below-market interest for a limited number of years. This type of mortgage may be necessary in order to qualify for financing with a specific lender. After the stated period expires, the interest rate rises to a predetermined level or converts to an adjustable rate. The developer may compensate the lender for its lost revenues from the buy-down agreement and offsets that expense by increasing the price of the home.

cap A limitation on the interest or payment the lender may charge in an adjustable-rate mortgage. A rate cap limits the interest rate increase per year and for the life of the contract. The less desirable payment cap limits the amount of monthly payment the borrower will be required to make, regardless of the effective interest rate. When the maximum payment is not adequate to cover a month's interest, the loan balance will increase rather than decrease, a condition known as negative amortization.

compound interest The method of computing interest based on the number of periods in a year. Annual compounding calls for a once-per-year calculation. Semiannual compounding involves twice-yearly interest payments at one-half the annual rate. Quarterly compounding involves four yearly periods at one-fourth the annual rate. Monthly compounding, the method in effect for the majority of mortgages, involves a calculation of interest on the outstanding balance, at 1/12th the annual rate. Daily compounding is figured on either 1/360th or 1/365th of the annual rate, with interest accruing every day.

conversion (1) The transfer of equity from the home buyer to the lender through payment of interest on a long-term loan. (2) The transfer of home equity to spending through refinancing or equity lines of credit.

creative financing Any form of financing other than a traditional mortgage calling for recurring payments of the same amount each month. Creative alternatives include balloon, buy-down, and graduating payment mortgages.

daily compounding A method of computing interest each day of the year. The method may involve calculation on the basis of a 360-day or 365-day year.

debt service The amount of money paid to a lender, involving the combined interest and principal for each period.

deferral rule A provision in federal tax law that a homeowner is not taxed on the profits from the sale of a principal residence to the extent that the individual reinvests in another home within two years before or after the sale date. If another home is built or purchased at a price below the sales price, the difference is taxed in the year of sale. The deferral cannot be claimed more than once in any two-year period.

effective tax rate The rate of tax that applies to taxable income each year. Taxable income is gross income minus adjustments, itemized deductions, and exemptions.

emergency reserve fund A fund of money set up in a savings account, money market fund, credit union account, or other highly available place. The purpose is to protect a family against unexpected expenses or financial problems.

equity That portion of a home that is free and clear of mortgage debt. Equity is created from the combination of the down payment, the market value of improvements, increases due to growth in market value, and principal payments made to the lender.

equity buildup The rate of growth in equity from repayment of a mortgage. On a 30-year fixed-rate loan, the buildup rate is very slow during the earlier years and accelerates toward the end of the loan term.

equity line of credit A line of credit granted by lenders and secured by the equity in a home. The homeowner may borrow up to the maximum allowed, which is usually 80 percent of the home's market value, less any outstanding loans. In many instances, the monthly repayment is scheduled for interest only, with the entire principal balance due at the end of a stated term.

exclusion rule A provision in federal tax law allowing homeowners aged 55 or older to exclude from tax up to $125,000 in profits from the sale of a home. The exclusion can be used only once.

first mortgage The mortgage having priority of claim in the event of foreclosure. Upon sale of the foreclosed property, the first mortgage will be repaid first; second mortgages and other liens will be satisfied from the remaining proceeds, if any.

fixed-rate mortgage A mortgage in which the interest rate is permanent for the entire term.

free and clear The condition of ownership in property when no mortgages or liens are owed.

full amortization Repayment of a loan on a schedule for a fixed number of years, with monthly payments designed to eliminate the principal balance by the end of the term.

graduating payment mortgage A mortgage in which the monthly payment is increased periodically, either by contract or as part of an accelerated payment plan. Additional payments are assigned to principal.

index loan A loan whose rate varies based on the changes in interest rates in an independent index.

interest-only loan Any loan in which monthly payments represent only the interest. The principal balance will become due at expiration of an agreed term of years.

level debt service A loan for which monthly payments do not change. For example, in a fully amortized 30-year loan, monthly payments are the same each month, but the split between interest and principal changes over time.

liquidity A condition of cash availability. In a savings account or money market fund, for example, investors can retreive their funds with little or no advance notice. In comparison, investing in home equity is highly illiquid, as funds can be taken out only by refinancing or committing to an additional mortgage.

loan relief A provision allowed by some lenders in which monthly mortgage payments are suspended for a limited period of time. During the suspension, interest continues to accumulate, so that a loan's balance rises each month.

market value The highest amount a buyer is willing to pay and that a seller is willing to accept for a property.

monthly compounding A method of compounding interest in which 1/12th of the annual rate of interest is applied against the previous balance of the loan. This method is the one most commonly used for mortgage loans.

mortgage constant A percentage derived by dividing the annual payments on a mortgage by the original loan balance. Lenders use the mortgage constant to describe the rate of repayment and yield. The shorter the mortgage term or the higher the level of acceleration, the higher the mortgage constant.

mortgage value The value set by a lender on a property for the purpose of evaluating risks associated with granting a loan. This value may be lower than the appraised or market value, because the lender will tend to view properties conservatively.

negative amortization A condition that may arise in an adjustable-rate mortgage with a payment cap. When the maximum monthly payment is lower than the amount of interest due, the loan's balance will rise as payments are made.

payment cap A provision in some adjustable-rate mortgages stating that the borrower will never be required to pay more per month than a stated maximum. However, the interest rate is not subjected to a cap; thus, interest costs could exceed the maximum monthly payment.

point A charge assessed by lenders upon granting a loan, as a form of additional interest. One point is equal to 1 percent of the loan balance.

prepayment penalty A penalty charged by the lender for repaying a mortgage in advance of the due date. Most mortgage contracts allow borrowers to repay a stated maximum per year without penalty, usually expressed as a percentage of the original loan.

principal That portion of the monthly payment that reduces the mortgage balance.

quarterly compounding A compounding method in which one-fourth of the annual rate is charged against the outstanding balance four times per year.

rate cap A form of cap in an adjustable-rate mortgage applied periodically and for the full term of the loan. Annual caps limit the amount of increase the lender is allowed to charge; overall caps limit the number of interest points the lender can assess above the starting rate.

refinancing The replacement of one loan with another, either for the same amount or for a greater amount of debt. Refinancing is one form of acceleration, when the rate of interest is lower with a new loan.

remaining balance tables Tables that show the percentage of the original loan that is due to the lender at the end of each year. The percentage varies depending on the interest rate and length of the original term.

renegotiated rate mortgage Alternate name for the balloon or rollover mortgage.

rollover mortgage Alternate name for the balloon or renegotiated rate mortgage.

second mortgage A mortgage that does not have a priority of claim against a foreclosed property, as does the first mortgage. Upon satisfaction of the first mortgage debt, holders of second mortgages and other liens will be repaid from any remaining funds.

secured debt Any borrowed money for which property is pledged as collateral for repayment. In the event of default, the borrower has the right to sell the pledged property to repay the loan.

semiannual compounding A compounding method in which one-half of the stated annual rate is assessed against the outstanding balance of a loan.

tax bracket The percentage of tax that is due based on taxable income. For example, an individual has taxable income on which 28 percent tax is due. That taxable income was derived after deducting itemized deductions and personal exemptions from adjusted gross income. The 28 percent rate is applied to the final taxable income, not to gross income earned.

tax deferral The delay of tax liabilities to a future period. This delay occurs whenever a principal residence is sold, and another home is built or purchased within two years that costs the same or more than the sales price of the previous home.

teaser Also called the *today rate*, a below-market interest rate charged by lenders to induce borrowers to accept an adjustable-rate mortgage. Within six months to one year, the teaser is removed and replaced with a much higher interest rate.

variable-rate mortgage Alternate name for an adjustable-rate mortgage.

INDEX

D

E

F

G

H

I

L